ENSURING SAFE SCHOOL ENVIRONMENTS

Exploring Issues—Seeking Solutions

TOPICS IN EDUCATIONAL LEADERSHIP
Larry W. Hughes, Series Editor

ENSURING SAFE SCHOOL ENVIRONMENTS

Exploring Issues—Seeking Solutions

Edited by

Mary Susan E. Fishbaugh
Montana State University–Billings

Terry R. Berkeley
Towson University

Gwen Schroth
Texas A&M University–Commerce

2003

LAWRENCE ERLBAUM ASSOCIATES, PUBLISHERS
Mahwah, New Jersey   London

Lawrence Erlbaum Associates, Inc., Publishers
10 Industrial Avenue
Mahwah, NJ 07430

Cover design by Kathryn Houghtaling Lacey

Library of Congress Cataloging-in-Publication Data

Ensuring safe school environments : exploring issues, seeking
    solutions / edited by Mary Susan E. Fishbaugh, Gwen
    Schroth, Terry R. Berkeley.

        p. cm.
Includes bibliographical references and index.
ISBN 0-8058-4310-8 (alk. paper)
1. School environment—United States. 2. School violence—
    United States—Prevention. 3. Schools—United States—
    Safety measures. I. Fishbaugh, Mary Susan. II. Schroth,
    Gwen. III. Berkeley, Terry R. IV. Series.
LC210.5 .E58 2002
371.7'82—dc21   2002018441
                                                      CIP

Books published by Lawrence Erlbaum Associates are printed
on acid-free paper, and their bindings are chosen for strength
and durability.

Printed in the United States of America
10 9 8 7 6 5 4 3 2 1

Appreciation and Dedication

The work of writing a book requires appreciation being
expressed to many. As a group, we are especially
appreciative of the support received from the authors of the
chapters in this work, many of whom were authors of articles
in the topical issue on School Safety published in *Rural Special
Education Quarterly* from which this book emerged.
The American Council on Rural Special Education
and its members have been especially supportive
for which we are most appreciative.

Personally, we dedicate this book to our children:
For MSEF: To Kate, Änna, Nik, and Geoff,
For TRB: To Anna,
For GS: To Peter.

Collectively, we dedicate this book to:

The victims of school violence and their families
who have suffered with such anguish,
the school personnel and members of the crisis teams
who provided strong support to so many,
and the communities in which they all live,
each striving to be more caring places.

Contents

Series Editor Foreword

Larry W. Hughes

In the past, one didn't think of schools to be dangerous places. But these later days are days of unrest, everywhere. And, days of courage too. School violence, just as any instance of violence in the nation and internationally, really is everyone's problem. And, in the instance of violence at school, the authors of this book make clear their insistence that everyone accept responsibility for making schools a safe environment. The problem is systemic.

Scott Poland, in his testimony of which chapter 1 is comprised, establishes the systemic framework. Poland provides a broadened perspective to the issue. His message is that "guns and metal detectors are merely small parts in solving the problem of school violence. In fact, society needs to reinvent itself." And, from the second chapter on, the basis for this "reinvention" is provided.

The volume is organized in two parts. In the first, the focus is on the issues themselves. A comparison is made between urban and rural school environments. A research base is presented; the school's principal's role is explored. The final chapter of Part I discusses the tensions, concerns, and problems with which the school leader is confronted on a daily basis.

The second part of the book focuses on solutions—what is being done and what else can be done. Included in this part are chapters on effective conflict management practices, behavioral support plans, school–community relations, the development of a caring school community as a way to decrease tendencies toward violence, and a model program, the Montana Behavioral Initiative, which provides an in-practice statewide program designed to demonstrate how to begin to develop a community-focused school.

The research base of this book is solid and the writers are knowledgeable about how schools and school communities operate. Thus, what is here is a book that has pertinence to school administrators, community leaders, and graduate students of school leadership. Much practical application is expressed. Of greatest importance is the need to see schools as a part of a community system—an organ, not a body itself. The issue of school violence is thus a systemic issue and that is the perspective the book reflects. It is also a perspective that requires complex processes to effectively address the problem. Those processes are the backbone of this book. Readers will find help here.

Preface

BACKGROUND

During March 1998, the American Council on Rural Special Education (ACRES) held its annual meeting in Charleston, South Carolina. ACRES is a small organization that emanated from a late-1970s federal grant to determine the effects of Public Law (PL) 94-142, the Education of the Handicapped Act of 1975, on special-education service delivery in rural America. In ACRES, there is a feeling of "family"—perhaps due to its size, its focus on rural, the consistency of its membership, and to the dedication of its members attending to the needs of children and families served in rural schools. Participants who attend an annual conference for their own aggrandizement rarely return. ACRES, then, is a professional organization with a good heart.

As ACRES members listened to keynote addresses, presented their sessions, and enjoyed the beauty of Charleston, there was a shooting of children in a Jonesboro, Arkansas, school by other children. These children lost their opportunity to gradually progress from a secure childhood to a productive adulthood. Two boys, not even teenagers, became nonchildren who would never be emotionally healthy adults. The children who were their victims would never be adults at all. This tragedy followed too closely similar tragedies and was not the last in a series of episodes of school violence shocking ACRES members at the conference and elsewhere.

The members serving on the ACRES National Board of Directors wondered what they could do in response to this latest incident of school violence. How could they support the bereaved to whom the members felt a kinship? Arkansas, after all, is a largely rural state. What was their responsibility as members leading a professional educational organization? The board members decided to take two steps—one was to adopt a policy statement in support of safe school environments in which children could grow and play and learn without fear, and the second was to dedicate a topical issue of its journal, the Rural Special Education Quarterly (RSEQ, 1998), to school violence.

ACRES' members felt so strongly about addressing school violence and supporting safe school environments that the editors of the topical issue proposed expanding that issue into a book. This volume is the result. Here, the journal articles have been rewritten to address safe schools from the perspective of suburban and urban, as well as rural environments. The text can be used as supplemental reading in courses preparing educators for their roles as school administrators as well as for administrators in other community-based human service agencies. It is appropriate for reflection by practicing school administrators and human services agency staff.

OVERVIEW

The text is divided into two parts. In Part I, Exploring Issues (chaps. 1–4), the focus is on issues. In Part II, Seeking Solutions (chaps. 5–9), solutions are offered for consideration by the reader. At the conclusion of each chapter there are questions and a case study to prompt further discussion. It is our hope as RSEQ topical issue editors, as text editors, and as members of ACRES, that this text will play a vital role in the preparation of school administrators whatever their setting, and it will be a part, however small, in restoring public trust in schools as safe havens for our children.

Chapter 1: Congressional Testimony: School Violence From the Perspective of a National Crisis Response Consultant

Chapter 1 sets the stage by presenting the compelling congressional testimony of Dr. Scott Poland, who has addressed the U.S. Congress on more than one occasion. The testimony referred to in this chapter took place in 1999 following incidents of school violence in Paducah, Kentucky, and Jonesboro Arkansas, but predated the tragedy in Littleton, Colorado. Dr. Poland's message remains the same—guns and metal detectors are merely very small parts in solving the problem of school violence. In fact, society needs to reinvent itself in order to prevent future incidents. Accepted violence in the media, in arcade games, in home-video games, and in other aspects of daily life seems to immunize youth to the realities of death and other acts of destruction. Alienation of youth from their peers and from their parents or other adults in a frenzied culture of hectic schedules, larger schools, and changing local mores has to be brought under control. Respect for each other among youth, respect for each other between youth and adults, respect for a necessary sense of community within society have to become the reality in which we live. School violence will stop only if we care about each other and demonstrate that caring with constancy.

Chapter 2: Comparison of Urban and Rural Conditions and Their Relationship to School Violence

Although the common perception that rural schools are immune to violence prevails, the authors of this chapter show this is far from the truth. The meaning of rural is changing because rural communities are no longer the generation-to-generation communities that they once were. Rural often, now, can equate to bedroom or commuter communities. Further, family farms and ranches are being sold to larger corporations. Rural students often attend large consolidated schools. The rural population is increasingly diverse. These changes mirror the urban environment where a mobile population, displacement of the workforce, large schools, and cultural/ethnic diversity can lead to alienation, unemployment, and misunderstanding. Urban and rural are not so different in their vulnerability for acts of youth violence.

Chapter 3: Decreasing School Violence: A Research Synthesis

Is research being conducted to determine causes and find successful responses or solutions to violence in schools? The authors present current efforts to discern both cause and response and suggest a direction for research without overwhelming the reader.

Chapter 4: Violence and School Principals

In this chapter the issue of safe/unsafe schools is presented to the school administrator or agency director, but other readers, such as classroom teachers and graduate students, will find it valuable as well. The following questions are posed and answered: What problems, tensions, and concerns are school principals (or agency directors) facing on a day-to-day basis? Increasingly, administrators are faced with belligerence, threats, and other negative behavior from parents. How, then, can children be taught nonviolence if their parents are modeling other behaviors? The reader can relate this chapter to the congressional testimony in chapter 1 and to the Violence Continuum presented in chapter 9. Ensuring safe school environments demands reduction of the societal acceptance of a culture of violence.

Chapter 5: Resolving Conflicts in Schools: An Educational Approach to Violence Prevention

This chapter presents step-by-step strategies for resolving conflicts in schools. If administrators, teachers, and students can learn better ways to live together, small conflicts do not have to escalate into violence or other antisocial behaviors.

Chapter 6: Creating Positive Behavior Support Plans for Students With Significant Behavioral Challenges

As more and more students with disabilities are included in non-special-education classrooms, all teachers will have to know how to work with them. This chapter addresses the behavioral issues of students with significant disabilities. The strategies proposed can also be applied to students with less obvious disabilities or without disabilities. For example, students with developmental disabilities (e.g., cognitive delay, autism or autism spectrum disorders, severe emotional disorders, multiple disabilities) often use behavior as a means of communication. Without understanding this, teachers and students often misinterpret such behaviors, and teachers punish students rather than trying to determine the purpose of the behavior in order to teach alternative acceptable means of achieving a goal or objective. In this chapter, the reader is introduced to the development and use of behavioral support plans.

Chapter 7: School–Community Relations: Policy and Practice

Schools are a part of society where each part impacts what happens in the others. Schools and the immediate community environments in which they are located must work hand in hand. This chapter suggests policies regarding school violence and its prevention and provides methods of policy implementation.

Chapter 8: Peaceable School Communities: Morality and the Ethic of Care

In this chapter, the ethic of caring is presented along with a discussion of how this ethic can be incorporated into schools. The authors suggest that a model of caring, of ethical consideration, of building community in schools should replace the production-based model that has prevailed in American Public Schools. Schools, they believe, need to foster the development of caring learners to prevent and decrease violence in schools and in modern society.

Chapter 9: The Montana Behavioral Initiative: Statewide Response to Issues of School Violence

The Montana Behavioral Initiative (MBI) is a statewide initiative developed to transform adversarial relationships between students and staff into a respectful milieu built by everyone who is a part of the school community. In this chapter the MBI is described, allowing the reader to begin to think about how to develop a positive, community-focused school.

ACKNOWLEDGMENTS

We'd like to think the LEA reviewers, Frederick C. Wendel from the University of Nebraska—Lincoln, and Cynthia J. Norris from the University of Tennessee.

REFERENCE

ACRES. (1998). Ensuring school safety [topical issue]. Rural Special Education Quarterly, 19(4).

I

EXPLORING ISSUES

1

Congressional Testimony: School Violence From the Perspective of a National Crisis Response Consultant

Scott Poland
Cypress-Fairbanks Independent School District, Houston, TX

This chapter includes two moving statements from Dr. Scott Poland, a man who is often first on the scene in response to school crises. Dr. Poland counsels those who have witnessed school violence and attempts to ameliorate the resulting trauma. We have included his statements because they are to the point, yet very caring. The existence of violence in schools, once considered the safest places for children to be during the day, is frightening and real.

BIOGRAPHICAL SKETCH

Scott Poland is Director of Psychological Services for the Cypress-Fairbanks Independent School District in Houston, Texas. The Department of Psychological Services in this district of nearly 70,000 students has received several state and national awards for excellence in providing psychological services during the 21 years Dr. Poland has served as director.

Past president of the National Association of School Psychologists (NASP), he has served several terms as chairman of NASP's National Emergency Assistance Team (NEAT), and has led or served on crisis teams in the aftermath of 10 school shootings throughout the United States.

Author of four books and numerous articles and chapters on the subject of school safety, crisis planning, and violence prevention, his writings have been translated into Chinese, Italian, and Japanese. Translations are in progress for both Turkish and Greek.

PHILOSOPHY OF NONVIOLENCE

School safety is an inside job that most importantly requires a commitment from the students and then from the faculty and the community. Much as been written about school violence in recent years, but government figures indicate schools are actually the safest places for children to be, and only 1% of youth homicides occur on school grounds. Dr. Poland believes that even one violent death at school is unacceptable, and schools must work on prevention. In addition, we must have prevention programs in place in our homes, neighborhoods, and communities. Children are dying in record or near-record numbers from accidents, homicides, and suicides. Prevention programs that address each of these leading causes of death to children are available and must be implemented.

The origins of youth violence are well known in our society and consist of the following:

- Child abuse.
- Ineffective parenting.
- Media violence.
- Violence in the home.
- Poverty.
- Prejudice.
- Substance abuse.
- Gun access.

These origins cannot be addressed by schools alone and must involve a commitment and allocation of resources at the local, state, and national levels.

There are some very positive initiatives at the federal level, especially in reports from the U.S. Surgeon General on the important topics of children's mental health, youth violence, and suicide prevention.

LESSONS LEARNED FROM EXPERIENCES

There is growing awareness by school administrators that school violence could occur at their school. Schools and local police are communicating more and especially have worked on clarifying procedures should a crisis occur. Many school administrators are providing local police with floor plans of schools and other important information that would be needed in a crisis situation. Several schools have clarified staff responsibilities in a crisis and have created "crisis boxes," which contain necessary information and supplies that would be utilized should an evacuation be necessary.

School personnel must be prepared for three waves of people to descend on a school after a crisis: police and medical, parents, and media. Planning and preparation will be necessary to manage those waves and to attend to the emotional as well as physical needs of staff and students. School administrators have a tendency to underestimate the initial and long-term impact of trauma. Children's reactions to trauma typically fall into the following key areas:

- Fear of the future.
- Academic regression.
- Behavioral regression.
- Nightmares and sleeping difficulties.

Classroom teachers and mental health professionals need to ensure that children are given permission for a range of emotions and are provided with opportunities to talk about the crisis incident, write about it, and express emotions through artwork, music, projects, and rituals. The adults in the school community also are affected and these school personnel have commented that they too need processing opportunities and support. Teachers and parents who are provided with emotional support and who are educated on children's typical reactions to trauma will be much better prepared to assist their students and children.

Adolescents, in particular, who have been traumatized are now more at risk for depression, suicide, reckless behavior, and substance abuse. The mental health services provided by professionals in schools are extremely inadequate. The personnel who typically provide these services are school psychologists and school counselors, but school psychologists spend the majority of their time conducting special-education evaluations and school counselors are extensively involved in scheduling and clerical duties.

A positive development is that the U.S. Congress appropriated $10 million for Project S.E.R.V. (Schools Emergency Response to Violence). The crisis teams that Dr. Poland led in San Diego in the spring of 2001 following school shootings were funded by Project S.E.R.V. Funding was provided for initial, as well as both short- and long-term mental health assistance (up to 13 months) for staff and student who were affected. The U.S. Department of Education organizes and directs these services.

The U.S. Secret Service released an interim report on school violence in the fall of 2000 in cooperation with the U.S. Department of Education, and it has been Dr. Poland's privilege to consult with the authors of that report. The report, based on their study of 37 school shootings, contains many key points, a few of which are:

- The perpetrators told other students of their violent plans.
- The majority of the perpetrators were bullied.
- The majority of the perpetrators were suicidal.
- Schools should have threat assessment teams.

Each of these key points has obvious implications for prevention.

The governor's task force on Columbine (Colorado) also released its findings in the spring of 2001. This report contains four major points:

- Columbine school personnel should have been more aware of impending violence.
- Local police should have been more aware of impending violence.
- The local police, who merely established a perimeter initially even though the shooting was in progress, should have acted more aggressively to stop the shooting and to help those who were injured.
- Schools should have a threat assessment team composed of (at a minimum) an administrator, a teacher, and a mental health professional, and the purpose of the team is to evaluate threats.

CONGRESSIONAL TESTIMONY INVITATION

Serving on or leading national crisis teams in the aftermath of 10 school shootings has given Dr. Poland a unique perspective. Having authored his first book on this subject in 1989, he has a long history of writing about personal experiences. The U.S. Congress has invited his testimony on three occasions in 1998, 1999, and 2001. These invitations were the result of Dr. Poland's leadership positions within his school system as well as in other positions and experiences at the state and national levels. For example, he served on the U.S. Department of Education's national assessment team that advised school officials after the 1995 bombing in Oklahoma City.

During his 1998 testimony before the U.S. Congress, he was surprised that a congressman asked how we could spot troubled children with the implication that the process was a mystery. His response was that school personnel identify them every day, but that insufficient mental health resources exist to provide the needed mental health interventions. The 1999 testimony was shortly before the Columbine tragedy and the hearing on school violence was sparsely attended and seemed to be a low priority. Dr. Poland asked those in attendance what had changed and why would we not expect youth violence and school violence to continue. The third testimony offered in the summer of 2001, was a briefing for the 67-member bipartisan children's caucus, with a focus on the impact of bullying and proposed legislation to provide more mental health workers in the schools. Upon arrival at the Capitol, Dr. Poland was notified that he would be not only testifying but moderating the briefing. Again, attendance, especially that of Republican legislators, was disappointing.

Several messages Dr. Poland continually and strongly emphasizes concerning school violence are:

- Violence can be prevented.
- Prevention efforts must address the origins.
- Students themselves must become more involved by serving on school safety committees.
- We must also end the conspiracy of silence that allows guns to be in schools and homicidal and suicidal threats to go unreported.

This will certainly be a difficult task, because young people typically do not report threats of violence for the following reasons:

- They have been conditioned not to tell.
- They fear retaliation.
- They do not want to get involved.
- They think that it could not or will not happen.

The enormity of the task of ending the conspiracy of silence was again evident when Dr. Poland spoke at the governor's conference on school violence in Oklahoma. Students in attendance had computer keypads to answer questions following each presentation. Fifty percent of the boys and 45% of the girls indicated that they would not report a gun on campus to an adult. This response poses a considerable challenge, thus, school safety solutions will not be easy to achieve. Solutions will have to involve a balance of hardware measures, such as more police and surveillance cameras, and more nonhardware measures like curricular programs to manage anger, learn to appreciate others, and reduce bullying, and increasing the availability of extracurricular programs for all students and not just those who are gifted in athletics.

The trend of school districts having massive high schools is particularly troubling. Texas, for instance, has 265 5A high schools, and student population at many of these schools is more than 3,000. Dr. Poland's daughter attends a high school of 3,600 students. With this large population, students often feel anonymous, are unable to participate in highly competitive extracurricular activities, and as a result become alienated from experiencing any sort of community in their day-to-day high school environment. Such alienation can lead to frustration and a violent response.

CONGRESSIONAL TESTIMONY—MARCH 1999

My name is Dr. Scott Poland and I am the Director of Psychological Services for the Cypress-Fairbanks Independent School District in Houston, Texas. I have been a school psychologist for 20 years, and crisis intervention and prevention has been the highest professional priority in my school system. I have authored several books and chapters on this subject and have provided training sessions for school personnel around the country. I am here today representing the National Association of School Psychologists (NASP), an organization of 21,000 school psychologists who promote educationally and psychologically healthy environments for all children and youth. I serve on the National Advisory Board for the National Association for Victim Assistance (NOVA). NASP and NOVA have formed a very rewarding professional alliance. National Emergency Assistance Team members served on 12 national crisis teams with NOVA in the past 18 months, including providing intervention after the tragic school shooting in Paducah, Kentucky; Jonesboro, Arkansas; Edinboro, Pennsylvania; and Springfield, Oregon.

There are indications that the actual number of violent acts and homicides by young people has declined. I am very pleased that is the case, but we still have a tremendous problem. Schools are much safer for children than the community, but I believe that one violent death in a school in our country is unacceptable. There has not been a school shooting that has horrified the nation this school year, as there were last year, but violent deaths at school have occurred this year in numerous locations around the country.

I served as the team leader of the National Crisis Teams sent to Paducah, Kentucky, and Jonesboro, Arkansas, following school shootings last year. These two communities asked NOVA to provide assistance. I have personally seen the pain and intense emotionality in Paducah and Jonesboro. The day after the shooting in Jonesboro, I faced a crowd of over 500 parents and students who were angry that the laws in Arkansas do not allow a lengthy incarceration for the youthful perpetrators. These parents and students were also tortured by the questions about why and how the shooting occurred, and why children are killing children. The NOVA team met with students, teachers, and parents of the families of the deceased and injured. We provided processing sessions not only at the school but at the hospital, police stations, and in the churches. It is clear that the path of the communities of Jonesboro and Paducah has changed and things will never be the same. I received a great deal of attention for my work in those two communities and I have had the opportunity to talk to many important people including President Clinton, Attorney General Reno, Secretary of Education Riley, and members of Congress last year. I never want to lose sight of the fact that in these two communities alone, seven fine young girls and their teacher died. I am absolutely committed to prevention and believe that it is time that our country made changes. My role as team leader in Paducah and Jonesboro provided me the opportunity to meet media representatives from around the world who were stunned that the United States, which we believe to be the best country in the world, has shootings at school, and as a nation we have done very little about it. The headline of *Newsweek* magazine on March 2, 1992 read: "Kids and Guns: A Report From America's Classroom Killing Grounds." My question is, "What have we done about this problem since March 1992?"

I have been asked many times why these school shootings have occurred and why there seems to be an increase in the problem of youth violence. The answer is a complex one, but I believe that we must recognize some things about young people today and make some very dramatic changes. I would like to outline several points:

1. Many young people do not understand the finality of death. Psychological theorists have outlined that by about age 13, children are in the advanced stages of intellectual development and should understand the permanence of death, and that death is a biological process. Twenty-five years of working with children have taught me that all children and even many adolescents do not understand the finality of death.

2. Young people are very influenced by the extreme violence that is portrayed on television, in movies, and video games. Dr. David Grossman of Jonesboro, a psychologist and former military colonel, has authored articles emphasizing that media influences have taught our children to kill. Research is being conducted by members of American Psychological Association and National Association of School Psychologists regarding the effects of television and motion picture violence on young people. The U.S. Supreme Court just this week refused to free the filmmakers of the movie *Natural Born Killers* from a lawsuit that accuses them of intentionally inciting copycat crimes. I believe that many times children who commit violent acts are simply carrying out what they see on television or at the movies. Our society glamorize violence. Many children also see violent acts in their homes and neighborhoods and believe that through violence you can get your way. We must reduce violent behavior that is modeled for young people not only through the media but in our homes, schools, and communities.

3. We must reduce gun availability to children. There are approximately 5,000 gun deaths to children under the age of 18 each year in America. There is a gun in every third home and almost every child can obtain a gun in a few hours. We are all very aware of the dramatic rise in the homicide and suicide rates for children during the last several decades.

I raise the following questions: Are children today that much more angry than children 30 years ago? Were the members of this committee concerned about another child or teenager shooting someone out of anger when you were in school? I think we all know that arguments between children used to be settled with fists. I do not condone fighting, but it was very rare to have a serious injury! The trigger pulls the finger! An angry child who has access to a gun will use it because it is there and it is in that child's hands. I realize that gun control is a complex issue in our country, but I also know that guns represent the single greatest threat to educators and school children.

I have personally counseled the victims of youth violence and youth suicide. I have had many conversations with parents where I pleaded with them to remove guns from the home of their homicidal or suicidal child. One father in the aftermath of his daughter's suicide with his pistol said, "But I thought that I taught all my children never to touch the pistol that I kept loaded on the dresser in my bedroom." Unfortunately, she used it to commit suicide. The good-bye note to her parents said, "Why did you make this so easy and make this gun so available to me?" The youth suicide rate is at or near an all time high; approximately 60% of youth suicides involve a gun.

I present crisis intervention information to school personnel regularly, and I raise questions about the need for guns in every third home in America and share statistics that show that a gun is more likely to kill a loved one through accident, homicides, or suicides than to be used to defend a home from an intruder. During the break at one presentation, I heard from two school custodians. The first one did not like my cautionary message about guns. The second custodian showed me that he had lost three fingers and had a scar on the side of his face where his ex-wife shot him in a moment of anger. He went on to comment that he no longer owned a gun.

I also support legislation that prosecutes adults when their gun is used by a child to injure or kill himself or someone else. We must increase penalties for adults who do not safeguard their guns from their children. In most states if your child uses your gun to injure or kill someone or himself, it is treated as a misdemeanor and the fine is comparable to a traffic ticket. We must increase penalties and prosecute to the fullest extent so all parents safeguard guns from children.

We must also develop and implement curriculum programs for all children that teach them about the effects of gun violence, how to identify, to avoid and to prevent situations that lead to gun violence. I compliment the school personnel in Dade County, Florida, who have developed a prevention program to reduce handgun death and injury to children. This program focuses on the danger of guns. Students hear from victims of gun death and injury themselves. The following tragic example illustrates the need for such programs: In Fall 1992, a Texas high school girl was angry at her boyfriend. She approached an adult neighbor and asked to borrow a handgun. The neighbor loaned it to her without questioning her as to why. She then fired the gun into the air to see if it worked. She got on the school bus with the gun (which was seen by numerous students) and made threatening remarks toward her boyfriend. She got off the bus, went to the cafeteria, and killed her boyfriend in front of many staff and students. One life was ended, another changed forever, and an entire school was victimized by violence. This example highlights several prevention points that involve the school and the community.

The following prevention strategies are recommended:

- Reduce gun availability to young people.
- Implement violence prevention, anger management, and problem-solving curriculum.
- Teach all students to report the presence of guns or any type of weapon on campus immediately and to report threats of violence.

I believe the single greatest strategy to reduce senseless tragic deaths of young people in our country is to reduce gun access to children under the age of 18 and to provide gun violence prevention programs in our schools and share them with parents and community members.

My experience after every school crisis has been that students always had many reasons to suspect homicidal or suicidal behavior. Many times friends or classmates were told very definite plans about homicidal or suicidal behavior. There are estimates that as many as 270,000 guns are taken to school each day in America. We must end the conspiracy of silence that allows guns, drugs, and other weapons in our schools. This will not be an easy task as evidenced by this example of one of the high schools in my own school district last May. A male student was carrying a gun in his backpack (he later said he had the gun for protection). As the bell sounded to end the day, he grabbed his backpack, the gun went off in the classroom, and a female student next to him was shot in the leg. She did recover from the serious injury. The next day I led the classroom discussion with those who witnessed the violence. The intervention seemed to be going well, but four students in a row said, "That was so serious; she could have been killed, and that could have been me! But you know what? *I don't think that I will tell an adult tomorrow if I saw a gun on campus!*" Not one student in the classroom disagreed publicly with that thinking. The teacher, counselor, assistant principal, and I could not convince the students of the need to tell the nearest adult. We have done a very poor job in our society of separating incessant tattling about inconsequential things from the need to tell about the presence of a gun on campus or homicidal and suicidal thoughts. We must begin to teach children at an early age through curriculum programs at every grade level that if they are feeling unsafe and especially if someone is talking about homicide or suicide, they must get adult help right away. I have had the chance to ask many educators at what age does it start that kids will not tell adults about serious situations such as a gun being on campus. The answer that I most often hear is that between third and fifth grades a major portion of children stop looking to adults for help. We must ensure that all children and adolescents know where to get adult help. This is an ambitious goal because ending the silence will involve many changes in churches, schools, and our families.

CHAPTER ACTIVITIES

For Discussion

1. Educational policy derives from the family of social policy. There are values upon which the policy rests. These values include (a) equity, (b) efficiency, and (c) choice. Describe these three values in the context of policy aimed at enhancing school safety and reducing school violence.
2. Who should be the beneficiaries of educational policy with a focus on school safety?
3. What benefits should accrue to these beneficiaries?
4. Because policy based on factual and empirical data may be more effective than policy based on speculation, what facts should be considered to enact policies with regard to school safety?
5. If the democratic process allows for the inclusion of emotion, how do/should facts and emotions interplay in development of policy related to school safety.

Case Study

Review newspaper archival reports about violence in Littleton, Colorado or more recently in San Diego, California. Write a synopsis of events beginning with the morning of the shooting and ending 1 week after the violence occurred. Analyze the incident using the following discussion points:

1. What school district policies and criminal/civil laws were in place in the community at the time of the violence? Were these laws adequate? Why or why not?
2. Should these policies have been more conservative, moderate, or liberal? Provide factual reasons for your position.
3. If laws regarding school safety are enacted, should they be enacted at the local, state, or national level? How might local needs demand modifications to laws enacted at higher governmental levels? Use Littleton as your local example.
4. Given the policies/laws in effect at the time of the incident, and given the extreme violence that occurred, how might you begin to evaluate the implementation of existing regulations?
5. In the first discussion question for this chapter, we stated that policy should be based on the values of (a) equity, (b) efficiency, and (c) choice. How do these values impact future policies with regard to school safety in the incident that you chose to review.

2

A Comparison of Urban and Rural Conditions and Their Relationship to School Violence

Gwen Schroth
Anita Pankake
Harry Fullwood
Gordon Gates
Texas A&M University-Commerce

> *Predatory crime does not merely victimize individuals, it impedes and, in the extreme case, prevents the formation and maintenance of community. By disrupting the delicate nexus of ties, formal and informal, by which we are linked with our neighbors, crime atomizes society and makes of its members mere individual calculators estimating their own advantage, especially their chances of survival amidst their fellows. Common undertakings become difficult or impossible, except for those motivated by a shared desire for protection.*
>
> —James Q. Wilson (1993, p. 26)

Current interest in and focused attention on the issue of violence in schools on the part of educators, parents, students, representatives of the media, business leaders, and academicians is understandable. Recent atrocities carried out by students in public schools in Colorado, California, Arkansas, and Oregon demonstrate the abilities of alienated students acting alone or in concert to engage in predatory behavior with horrific consequences. Feelings of distress, disgust, fear, and forlornment arise and threaten to tear further at an already besieged trust and waning confidence in America's educational system. Continued support for public education is essential for the survival of this institution considered by many to be the foundation of American democracy. Thus, developing an understanding of school violence is important and hopefully contributes to perspectives, policies, and programs that reduce or prevent the future occurrence of violent student behavior.

Studies of violent behavior by students in the school setting have become of general interest only recently so literature or developed theory on the topic is sparse. Attention to violence in rural schools receives even less attention than violence in urban settings. Discussions in the educational literature frequently borrow from criminology; however, criminologists are quick to identify the weaknesses in their own literature. Violence is deviance, and, as such, is fraught with many ethical, methodological, and operational difficulties.

We begin here by describing the communities and environments from which youth violence emerges and outline some recent changes that may contribute to what is happening in schools and communities today. To provide a complete background, urban settings are described first because this is where America's population is most highly concentrated and from where most research on violence originates. The next section, on rural America, is included for several reasons. First, it completes the picture; second, the rates of violence and crime are increasing most rapidly in rural areas; and, third, the myth exists that safety can be found in small, rural communities.

THE URBAN SCENE

According to the U.S. Census Bureau (1991), 3,067 counties exist in the United States. Of these, only 626 are classified as metropolitan; however, although the 626 represent only 20% of the total number of counties, these counties included 79% of the total U.S. population in 1990. Attention to these metropolitan areas regarding all facets of life—economic, social, educational, demographic, and so on—is a natural consequence of the large number of people residing there. Even though Hobbs (1994) asserted that "Times have blurred what were once clear distinctions between rural and urban America" (p. 6), when the topics are violence, crime, gangs, and concerns for the state of public education, urban centers still receive much of the attention.

Following a definition of urban and a presentation of some general demographic facts and figures, special attention is given to violence and crime in urban schools. Finally, what researchers and demographers offer as possible causes of crime and violence in the cities of this country are discussed.

Urban America

The metropolitan centers of the United States include both urban and suburban areas. The following facts provide a richer picture of the urban scene demographically, socially, economically, and geographically:

- All 50 states include at least one metropolitan area (Hobbs, 1994).
- Median family income inside metropolitan areas in 1997 was $39,383 compared to $20,400 outside metropolitan areas (U.S. Census Bureau, 1997).
- The central cities of the nation's largest urban areas have much higher rates of officially reported violence than are found in other areas (Hawkins, 1996).
- Approximately 75% of the U.S. population lived in urban areas, even though urbanized areas account for less than 2% of the national territory (*Encyclopedia Britannica Online*, n.d.).
- Another 15% of the population resided in areas that are less densely populated but are directly linked economically and/or socially to urban areas (*Encyclopedia Britannica Online*, n.d.).
- In the last 90 years, the average percentage of population in cities engaged in manufacturing dropped from 17.1% to 9.3% whereas the percentages for services rose from 20.0% to 27.3% (Sukkoo, 2000).

Metropolitan areas play a key role in the economic and demographic make-up of the United States. The population concentrations make a natural environment for social issues of every sort. Because every state has one or more metropolitan areas, the issues of urban America are of concern for everyone.

The United States has changed from being a predominantly rural to a predominantly urban nation. During the colonial period of our nation's development, 95% of the people lived in rural settings (*Encyclopedia Britannica Online*, n.d.). Today, however, nearly 80% of the people living in the United States reside in one of its 268 standard metropolitan statistical areas (Sukkoo, 2000; *World Book Multimedia Encyclopedia*, 1999). Knowledge of some of the economic, social, and demographic changes in urban areas helps in understanding how this setting fosters and sustains violence and crime.

Hobbs (1994) noted that "urban areas have continued to sprawl outward, making the boundaries of cities less and less distinct" (p. 6). Though cities still provide the focus for metropolitan areas, the spread of the population to close-in suburbs and other areas farther out results in making it more and more difficult to tell where the city ends and the country begins. As these population shifts occurred, even the terminology referencing urban American changed. Early references to city and country gave way to urban and rural. With continued growth and the improvements in transportation, people began to move outside the cities. These new rings of growth were called "suburbs." As suburban areas increased in number and distance from the central city, these combinations of central cities and suburban areas were dubbed metropolitan areas. The number of standard metropolitan areas (a core city and its surrounding urban and suburban populations) has increased from 168 in 1950 (Knezevich, 1984) to 268 in 1999 (*Encyclopedia Britannica Online*, n.d.).

Urban Schools

A major reason for attention to the problems of urban schools, particularly those related to crime and violence, is related purely to numbers. Stern (1992) offered the following figures based on information from the U.S. Department of Education: "Total enrollment in U.S. schools is 40,501,948; 61.7 percent of those students are enrolled in urban/suburban schools; 21.8 percent are enrolled in school in small towns; and only 16.5 percent of U.S. students are enrolled in rural schools" (p. 73). Because close to two-thirds of U.S. students attend school in urban/suburban areas, research and opinions about the problems of education often reference the schools in the nation's metropolitan areas. Urban schools are described as follows:

- Large, impersonal places in which students have lower achievement levels than students in suburban or rural areas (U.S. Department of Education, 1994).
- Settings where high rates of school dropout occur, regardless of race, but significant dropout problems exist among ethnic minority students (Huelskamp, 1993). (Nearly 80% of White students complete high school on time; only 70% of Black students and 50% of Hispanic students graduate as scheduled.)
- Places that serve greater numbers of ethnic minority students than schools outside the cities. "Almost half (49%) of urban students belong to a racial or ethnic minority, compared with 21% of suburban students and 16% of rural students" (Center for the Future of Children, 1997, p. 137).
- Locations in which students either hide their interest in academics or give up any such pursuits altogether because of the nonsupportive culture of their peers or the school neighborhood.

An important change impacting urban schools is the shrinking American White population (Hodgkinson, 1999). This population is now a minority in virtually all of the nation's largest city systems and in a growing number of smaller ones as well (Kantor & Brenzel, 1993). "By 2020, half of all U.S. students ages 0–18 will be nonWhite. By 2050, half of all Americans will be 'minority.' Hispanics and Asians will account for 6 percent of U.S. population growth between 1995 and 2025—44 percent Hispanic and 17 percent Asian" (Hodgkinson, 1999, p. 13).

The Changing Urban Scene

Two major changes in urban America directly and indirectly influenced the rates of violence among youth. First is the severe economic shift, which included declines in economic production bases, revenue for support of city services, and individual family income. Prior to 1900, the economic focus of the city was on the production, collection, and distribution of physical commodities and basic services. More recently, a shift toward production and consumption occurred that focused more heavily on services, especially knowledge, managerial, and recreation industries. Cities are now more dependent on corporate headquarters, communication industries, and the manipulation of information as their economic building blocks (*Encyclopedia Britannica Online*, n.d.; Sukkoo, 2000).

Prior to the 1950s, people living in the suburbs still considered the central city as their workplace; however, with increasing frequency over the last 30+ years, businesses and industries have located in the suburbs. Those who live in the suburbs now also work, attend cultural and social events, and buy needed goods and services in the suburbs rather than the city (*World Book Multimedia Encyclopedia*, 1999).

An important economic consequence of these shifts was a decline in property values and the tax revenues. Though many people in the suburbs take advantage of parks, museums, sports arenas, and theaters Located in the central city, they live outside the taxing area that supports them (*World Book Multimedia Encyclopedia*, 1999). This shift in tax revenues strongly impacts inner-city school financing. According to Burrup, Brimley, and Garfield (1993):

> When property taxes were the main source of school revenue and state allocations were minimal, city school districts usually enjoyed certain revenue advantages. City school boards tended to be less vocal in their opposition to property tax increases for education than their rural counterparts. As a consequence, city schools generally outdid their rural neighbors in providing good education and became known as the leaders in administrative efficiency and in student achievement. In recent years, however, the pattern has changed. Gradual changes in the socioeconomic makeup of larger cities, with consistent emigration of the more affluent to suburbia, have resulted in cities losing much their previous advantage. Legislative bodies that once faced the formidable problem of financing small rural schools equitably now face a larger problem in providing adequate and equitable revenue for urban districts. (pp. 138–139)

The economics of families as well as businesses are shifting. According to *World Book Multimedia Encyclopedia* (1999) income and social status increase as the distance from the core of the city increases. U.S. Census Bureau statistics (*World Book Multimedia Encyclopedia*, 1999) on comparison of median income of individuals inside metropolitan areas and those outside metropolitan areas demonstrate some interesting insights regarding individual economics of the city. Median income for individuals living inside metropolitan areas is offered as $39,381 whereas for those outside metro areas it is $30,057; however, more important is the subdivision of those in the metro area into inside the central city and outside the central city. With that disaggregation, the income of the central cities begins to mirror the income of those outside the metropolitan area; that is, inside the central city 1997 income was reported as $31,548 and 1997 income for those inside the metropolitan area but outside the central city was $44,668. With the move of businesses to the suburbs, fewer employment opportunities are available for those who remain as residents in the central city.

A second major change in urban areas is the racial composition of the population due to out-migration. In a lecture entitled "The Changing Face of Education: Urban Schools in the New Millennium," Simmons (1999), director of the Annenberg Institute for School Reform, stated that demographically, society is changing rapidly in urban communities and schools. Urban school districts today form 7% of the districts in the nation, enroll 24% of the nation's students, but serve 43% of its minority students. As an example of the population shift, Simmons cited figures from one district showed that a decade ago White students made up 40% of the district's population whereas Latinos accounted for 20%, figures that now are reversed.

A major reason for individuals and families to move to the suburban areas was to avoid the crime, housing shortages, and racial conflicts of the city. However, crime rates outside inner cities are growing so rapidly that suburban and rural areas are no longer havens of safety (Donnermeyer, 1994).

Violence in Urban Communities

In 1991, the crime rate in urban America was 6,492 incidents per 100,000 persons, a rate that is three times higher than the crime rate in rural areas (Donnermeyer, 1994). Wright, Sheley, and Smith (1992) lamented that "Incidents that would have seemed shocking and inexplicable just a few years ago—gang warfare, drive-by slayings, wanton brutality, in-school shootings—have somehow become commonplace in urban existence" (p. 84). Wright, Sheley, and Smith surmise that:

> Center-city minority and underclass neighborhoods have become remarkably unsafe because decades of indifference to the social and economic problems of the cities has bred an entire class of people, especially young people, who no longer have much stake in their future. Isolation, hopelessness, and fatalism, coupled with the steady deterioration of stabilizing social institutions in the inner city and the inherent difficulties of maintaining security through normal agents of social control, have fostered an environment where "success" implies predation and survival depends on one's ability to defend against it. (p. 89)

In 1978 the Vocational Foundation in New York City produced a white paper entitled "Our Turn to Listen" that revealed the following:

> Across the country, ghetto youths are between 10 and 20 times more likely than other young people to be arrested for violent offenses—from assault to

murder…. There are nearly 2 million unemployed teenagers in America, Black and White, comprising nearly one-fifth of the labor force between the ages of 15 and 19. In the ghettos, however, minority youths have an official unemployment rate of 44 percent; the Urban League suggests the real number is 60 percent (pp. 9, 13)

Based on National Crime Statistics data, the less educated have higher rates of violence no matter the location; additionally, people of lower income in all geographic areas exhibit higher rates of violence (Donnermeyer, 1994). Similarly, alcohol and drug abuse incidents are similar for urban and rural youth except that the urban youth are more likely to be users of cocaine and cocaine derivatives (Donnermeyer, 1994).

Violence in Urban Schools

After reviewing a study conducted by the Centers for Disease Control and Prevention (CDC) on youth risk behavior, Green (1999) stated, "Violence in our schools is a dreaded reality for the entire nation. In three years, adolescent males have shot and killed more than 30 students in multiple homicides at schools. As the incidence of violence climbs, students across the country are feeling unsafe at school" (p. 17). Results from the study by the CDC revealed:

- 8.5% of high school students carried a weapon (gun, knife, or club) on school premises during the 30 days preceding the survey.
- Slightly over 7% of high school students were threatened or injured with a weapon on school property during the 12 months preceding the survey.

According to Prothrow-Stith (1995), "Our poorest adolescents have armed themselves and become guerrilla fighters against each other in a way that has no logic and no political ideology, with no end in sight" (p. 97). And, as Gorski and Pilotto (1995) observed, "In some cities, schools are no longer neutral zones nor a safe egalitarian haven for children. Traditionally, the school has always been a reflection, and extension, and a formalization of the predominant values of the community and society in which it resided" (p. 2).

The disintegration of the traditional family and its values, and the apathy, disorganization, and hostility of the once close-knit neighborhood are mirrored in the schools. Both teachers and students appear justified in fearing for their own safety with the consequence that the learning process is stymied by the need to deal with unruly behaviors and to prevent serious episodes of aggression and violence (Gorski & Pilotto, 1995). A 1994 National School Boards Association (NSBA) study found the following:

- 82% of the 720 school districts surveyed reported an increase in violence.
- 78% of the increases were made up of student-on-student assaults.
- 28% of the increases were from student-on-teacher attacks.

Prothrow-Stith's (1994) comments reinforce these findings: "Almost 3 million crimes occur on or near school property each year. An estimated 400,000 students were victims of violence at school in a recent six-month period. Violence is the second leading cause of death for America's students" (pp. 8–9).

According to Takata (1994), "Gangs are a fact of life in today's American cities" (p. 95). The presence of gangs represents a major difference between violence in urban and rural areas. The following facts and figures highlight the problem:

- 8% of the students living in rural areas indicate that gangs are active in their school (Takata, 1994).
- Students reporting gang activity in their schools increases to 14% in suburban areas and climbs to 25% for students in city schools (Takata, 1994).
- The number of school-age gang members is especially high in urban areas where poverty, crime, and isolation of ethnic populations is the norm (Riester & Deegear, 1997).

Violence in schools is not a new phenomenon. As early as 1978 a study entitled "Violent Schools—Safe Schools: The Safe School Study Report to Congress/Executive Summary" (National Institute of Education, 1978), sponsored by the U.S. Department of Health, Education, and Welfare, in which 4,000 elementary and secondary schools were surveyed revealed that:

- 40% of robberies and 36% of assaults on urban youth took place in schools.
- Approximately 8% of schools had serious problems of crime, violence, and disruption.
- About 3 million secondary students avoided certain places in their schools out of fear, and about half a million students were afraid at school most of the time.
- About 125,000 high school teachers were threatened with physical harm each month and reported being reluctant to confront misbehaving students, and half of all the teacher respondents said that they have experienced verbal abuse in a typical month.

Ten years later, in 1989, Menacker, Weldon, and Hurwitz conducted research in the Chicago public schools similar to the Violent Schools—Safe Schools study and discovered the following:

- More than 50% of the students reported that money, clothing, or personal property was stolen from them at least once during the school year, and 35% indicated that thefts occurred more than once.
- 8% of the students said they were threatened by someone with a gun or knife who wanted money or drugs, and 3% reported that they had been threatened more than once.
- 7% of the students admitted coming to school high on drugs or alcohol at least once during the year.
- 32% of the students said they had carried a weapon to school at least once, and 14% said they had done so more than once.
- 15% of the students admitted hitting a teacher at least once during the year.
- 42% of the teachers said they hesitated at least once to confront misbehaving students out of fear for their own safety.

According to Futrell and Powell (1996), the figures on violence in the 1990s show that the possibility that a disagreement among students will be settled with some type of weapon rather than an old-fashioned fistfight has increased significantly. "A major difference between violence in the schools in the 1950s and the 1990s is the presence and use of weapons, especially guns. Also, students seem to hold a grudge much longer. Some students wait until the last day of school to settle an incident that occurred weeks or months earlier" (p. 1). In an NSBA survey of more than 1000 administrators, 54% of suburban and 64% of urban school officials reported more violent acts in their school in 1993 than 5 years before (National School Boards Association, 1994).

After reviewing the findings from studies over the last 20 years, conclusions about crime and violence in urban schools seem to relate to the number, the types, and the severity of incidents. All types of crimes appear to be on the increase—theft, harassment, illegal drug use, assault, and use of deadly weapons. The severity of the crimes and the frequency with which they occur also seem to be increasing. More thefts are committed and the costs involved are greater. Physical threats are more frequent and an increase in incidents that actually result in physical assaults are also seen. Carrying and using weapons (knives and guns) are reported more often by those who commit crimes and by those who wish to protect themselves from crimes. Additionally, the adults in schools are fearful of violence from the students; sadly, these individuals who historically were the keepers of the schools as havens of safety for children are themselves now victims and potential victims of crimes committed by children.

The changing face of violence points to questions about the origins of school crime and violence. Did crime come to the school from the outside or have students now taken their in-school crimes to the streets and the neighborhoods surrounding their schools? What are the causes? Answers to these questions will be essential if any viable solutions to these problems are to be proposed and implemented.

CAUSES OF URBAN VIOLENCE

Prothrow-Stith (1994) asserted that the causes of violence are complex and woven into our culture. She identified a variety of elements that interact in creating the complex culture of violence; among them are poverty, racism, drugs and alcohol abuse, unemployment, low wages in the inner city, gangs, access to guns, regulation of handguns, and family violence. She is not alone in her assessment of the complexity of causes for violence. Johnson and Johnson (1995) lamented that, "What is perhaps most alarming is that violence is becoming so commonplace in many communities and schools that it is considered the norm rather than the exception" (p. 3). A number of factors that contribute to urban violence are discussed in the literature. Those that are most widely discussed are addressed here.

Social and Academic At-Risk Factors

Prothrow-Stith (1995) pointed out that some children are more at risk than others. The risk factors she identified include being male, being poor, residing in an urban area, and being a witness to or victim of violence during early development. With regard to poverty as a risk factor, Prothrow-Stith noted that one in five children live in poverty—3.4 million nationwide. Repeatedly, a strong association is found between failing in school and delinquent behavior. Poor grades, low achievement, retention in grade, and failure to attain basic skills in reading, writing, and mathematics all contribute to students' dislike for and poor attitude toward school. Students with these difficulties and the resulting attitudes are more likely to demonstrate delinquent behaviors (Brier, 1995). With such frequency of school failure, a rich context for delinquent behaviors is formed.

Gangs

According to Riester and Deegear (1997), the number of school-age gang members is particularly high in urban areas. Urban areas are often poor, have high crime rates, and exist in settings of ethnic isolation. Reister and Deegear asserted that there is evidence to show that gangs and delinquent behavior flourish in neighborhoods where other social institutions have declined, where unemployment is high, and where families have become dysfunctional and overburdened, that is, in urban (central-city) America. The problem of gangs is so common in the urban areas that schools have developed their own departments to address these problems. Such units work with local police departments both to deal with the crimes committed by gangs and to prevent gang affiliations by offering youth alternative affiliations. Gangs offer youth social identity and economic opportunities that traditional institutions such as schools, families, and employment no longer offer in central cities (Lockwood, 1993; "Youth Violence," 1997).

At one time gangs were seen as a concern only in central cities. Now, however, "gangs have spread their networks, based mostly in larger cities, to encompass smaller cities and even rural communities" ("Youth Violence," 1997, p. 3). Consequently, as Takata (1994) declared, "Gangs are a fact of life in today's American cities" (p. 95).

Availability and Use of Weapons

"Gunfire kills 15 individuals under the age of 19 daily (Johnson & Johnson, 1995, p. 2). Wright et al., (1992) found that high percentages of inner-city youth had or were able to get a firearm. Generally, these youth grew up in families where carrying a firearm was a part of normal behavior, not some aberrant or exceptional behavior. The research even revealed established preferences regarding criteria for weapons including firepower, taceability, quality of construction, ease for shooting, and accurateness. Wright et al. noted that in some central-city neighborhoods carrying a gun is an established part of the culture. They asserted that even if urban environments become safer, elimination of weapons would take time. They concluded, "Whether predator or prey, the larger urban environment encourages one to be armed" (p. 89).

Demise of Social Institutions

Riester and Deegear (1997) found that gangs often flourish in areas where social institutions are absent. Families are stressed and overburdened, legal employment opportunities are disappearing, and schools are distant in relationships and disasters in academic achievements. In a review of parenting practices and school violence, Futrell and Powell (1996) found that teachers report about students, even young students, who state that their parents have told them (the children) that they do not have to do what the teacher says. Johnson and Johnson (1995) cited social conditions as supportive of the increased violence of adolescents. Among their concerns are divorce, abuse, poverty, and drugs. They also emphasized the separation of workplaces from neighborhoods as taking adults away from their children. This separation, in turn, they said, creates isolation from the necessary socialization that children need to learn about the norms of society. They concluded that "No one is teaching children how to manage conflicts constructively through example or through indirect methods, such as moral codes and patterns of living" (p. 3). Reinforcing this social context argument is Prothrow-Stith's (1994) assertion that a large proportion of violence occurs in families and between and among friends and acquaintances. She reported that, "Close to half of all homicides, a majority of the school fights, and all incidences of domestic violence occur between persons who know each other" (p. 96).

Prothrow-Stith's (1994) assertion used to introduce this section on causes of urban violence bears repeating as the section closes; that is, the causes of violence are complex and woven into the culture. The causes reviewed here range from individual difficulties such as learning problems, needs for social identity, and drug and/or alcohol dependency to societal issues of poverty, economic stability, and the decline of social institutions such as schools, churches, and families. Violence is pervasive in life in urban America; solutions to violence in urban America must be pervasive as well.

THE RURAL SCENE

One fourth of Americans reside in rural areas (Monsey, Owen, Zierman, Lambert, & Hyman, 1995). Though rural communities vary in architecture, agriculture, climate, and geographical features, a 1994 research report by the U.S. Department of Education's Office of Educational Research and Improvement points to some distinguishing characteristics of rural communities as a whole.

Characteristics of Rural Communities

Rural communities share some common characteristics that differentiate them from highly populated parts of the country. The 1994 U.S. Department of Education's report shows that rural America:

- Is sparsely populated, averaging fewer than 40 residents per square mile, and is located outside the effective commuting range of a metropolitan area.
- Has a higher poverty rate than urban areas, a rate that is rapidly increasing (Hodgkinson, 1994, refers to rural youth as the invisible poor).
- Sustains a jobless rate higher than metropolitan counties.
- Has a job and income growth rate that lags behind the rest of the nation.
- Provides jobs that require few skills and pay poorly.
- Has a rising rate of families headed by women.
- Is no longer supported by the farming industry.
- Experienced a dramatic exodus of breadwinners, particularly since 1980.
- Lags behind in opportunities for higher education and/or well-paying occupations. According to Hobbs (1994), this lack of opportunities "is both cause and effect for the continuing migration of the most highly educated youth from rural communities" (p. 18).

Although these figures on rural life with regard to poverty, joblessness, and dearth of skilled professions portray rural life as less than attractive, statistics indicate that urban families are moving to rural communities in growing numbers. Those who migrate to rural communities do so for several reasons. Rural schools are one of the attractions.

Rural Schools

According to the U.S. Department of Education's 1994 report, 46% of school districts in America are rural and are most likely to be in the north central, southern, and western parts of the United States. Schools in these rural districts generally:

- Have enrollments of fewer than 400 students and, in one out of five of these schools, have fewer than 100 students.
- Have student achievement levels that are generally higher than those of the disadvantaged urban youth but lower than those of the advantaged urban groups.

Low school enrollment rates is one of the attractions urban families find in rural settings. Another is that smaller schools provide a forum for more positive attitudes about school and closer connections between students and teachers than do urban schools ("School Size and Violence," 1999).

The influx of urban families has little impact on rural school funding. McLean and Ross (1994) pointed out that rural schools have small budgets with few government resources funneled their way. Although the school is the largest employer/financial institution in rural communities, fewer governmental resources are sent to rural than to urban schools. These funding inequities relate to inequities in the quality of education for rural and urban children. Some might argue that operating rural/small schools is less expensive than running large, urban schools, but a study of small, rural schools in Vermont showed that the per-pupil cost of operations ran about 18% higher than the state average ("Vermont Takes Positive Stand," 1999). Some of the funding inequities are attributed to a commonly held belief that rural schools do not have the problems of racism, violence, and general decay that more metropolitan schools have (Petersen, Beekley, Speaker, & Pietrzak, 1998).

The Changing Rural Scene

Historically, rural communities are portrayed as having two-parent families who sit down together to a home-cooked meal after the parents complete their work in the fields and the children return home from a trouble-free day at school. The church is a focal point in this picture—a place providing families spiritual comfort and opportunities for social support. "The family, the church, and the school have been at the heart of rural communities since this country was settled. These three institutions have provided the standards of behavior, circles of personal interaction, and a variety of social activities that collectively shape community ethos and identity" (U.S. Department of Education, 1994, p. 21).

In reality, this idyllic portrayal of rural life is changing. Rural churches and schools have lost considerable influence (Hobbs, 1994). The tight-knit rural family, traditionally viewed as a stabilizing influence on students and a strength of rural life, is also weakening. In a recent survey of school administrators, Stephens (1994) found that over 50% of the respondents felt that lack of parental involvement was the single most important contributor to school violence. In a study comparing schools of varying size (Petersen et al., 1998), 611 teachers and administrators were polled for their perceptions of school violence. No matter the size of the school, the perceived causes of violence were lack of family involvement and supervision of children, family violence, and instability and emotional atmosphere of the perpetrators' families. Teachers and administrators in the rural schools referenced the church, noting the low family involvement in moral/religious activities. The rural educators also reported that students' lack of trust/credibility in authority figures contributed to the rate of violent student behavior, factors not particularly noted by educators in suburban and urban schools. On the other hand, rural parents apparently continue to maintain a degree of control over their children. In a survey of 1,004 8th- and 10th-grade students in small central Texas communities, nearly 53% considered what their parents think to be the most important influence in keeping them from fighting (Kingery, Mirzaee, Pruitt, & Hurley, 1990). This vestige of parental influence over adolescents may contribute to the attraction urban parents find in rural communities.

Coupled with the changing nature of the rural family, school, and church is the economic restructuring of rural communities that undermines the traditional sense of belonging and reduces local control. Not only is the rural economy directly connected with national and international markets, but rural schools, health care, and other services are now a part of national systems. One consequence of these changes is greater rural community dependency and less autonomy. "It is increasingly difficult for rural residents to maintain a sense of community when so many things they depend on are located somewhere else" (Hobbs, 1994, p. 14).

Rural America can no longer be portrayed as it was 50 years ago. The traditional family farm, safe schools, and isolated communities are vanishing. What exists now is increasingly similar to and connected with urban centers.

Violence in Rural Communities

Violence in rural communities is still not fully comprehended or entirely explained. The clamor to understand youth violence is now raising questions that require answers, highlighting the need for increased research. A number of factors contribute to the dearth of information:

> One of the least understood topics in the fields of criminology and criminal justice today is that of rural crime. The reasons are simple. First, research on rural crime remains sparse. Scholars and researchers have spent most of their efforts trying to understand urban patterns of crime. Second, popularized images of rural and urban areas include stereotypes that contain elements of the truth, yet represent gross exaggerations of reality. The image of rural America today still suggests that small towns, farming communities, and the open country are "crime free." This perception is not accurate; yet, relative to the problems of some large urban communities, rural areas do look like havens of safety. (Donnermeyer, 1994, p. 27)

This continuing image of rural America as being "crime free" is attractive to some urban parents. Increasingly, those with sufficient means move their children into rural communities to flee the high rates of urban violence.

Though rural America can no longer be characterized as totally safe from crime and violence, in 1990 only 16% of all violent crime occurred in rural areas (Monsey et al., 1995). Yet the gap is closing. Donnermeyer in 1994 and Bachman in 1992 found that rural crime rates are increasing faster than those in urban areas: "From 1988 to 1991, rural rates have gone up 8.6 percent, compared to 3.6 percent for urban areas" (Donnermeyer, 1994, p. 31). Differences in substance abuse rates are similar; rural rates are increasing faster than urban (Hobbs,1994). A 1995 report on rural crime and violence by Monsey et al. found that from 1965 to 1992, rape, robbery, and assault rates in rural areas tripled.

In a close examination of the rural crime and violence, Monsey et al. (1995) found that (a) Whites more than Blacks are the victims, and (b) the perpetrator is usually a relative of the victim and is more likely to be drunk than are perpetrators in urban areas. Additionally, a 1990 Texas survey of 1,004 8th- and 10th-grade students from small Texas communities showed that, excepting school-supervised environments, "30 percent had been threatened with bodily harm though not actually hurt, and 16 percent had been physically attacked.... Eighteen percent said someone tried to force them to have sex when they did not want to" (Kingery et al., 1990, p. 24).

Violence in Rural Schools

The lack of data on violence in rural schools parallels the scarcity of information on violence in rural communities. One explanation for the scarcity is that rural educators are unwilling to recognize and document the severity of the problem. "Reports of violence in rural schools are few by contrast with those in urban and suburban schools, so the danger for potential violence may be perceived as 'not serious.' District personnel in rural America appear hesitant to acknowledge violence as a problem" (Bachus, 1994, p. 19). Consequently, school leaders all too often adopt a "wait-and-see" attitude.

Second, school incidents are not always acknowledged or reported because of educators' easy access to parents and relatives of students—social and familial relationships are closely intertwined. Thus, incidents of violence are disposed of informally and without documentation, which can foster false assumptions. "Because of the infrequency of published acts of violence in small schools, rural administrators, board members, and teachers are likely to feel safe" (Bachus, 1994, p. 19).

Educators' Concerns.   Despite the lack of research on rural school violence, one comparative study in particular is helpful. Petersen and a group of researchers (1998) investigated violence in school districts of varying sizes, representing Northwest, West, Midwest, South, East, and Northeast regions of the United States. The districts studied were then identified as urban, suburban, or rural. Teachers and administrators listed, in rank order, the 10 violence-related behaviors in their schools that increased the most in the past 2 years. These findings showed some similarities as well as differences between the three types of schools, urban, suburban, and rural:

- Student-to-student violent behavior was ranked the highest (10) in rural schools but third highest (7) in urban and suburban schools.
- The increase in biologically damaged children (i.e., fetal alcohol and crack babies) was ranked the highest (10) by urban and suburban educators.
- Incidents of fires/arson were listed by rural educators but not by urban and suburban teachers and administrators.
- Verbal intimidation/threats, pushing and shoving by students, and punching and/or hitting were ranked among the top four by all three groups.
- Sexual harassment was ranked higher by suburban and rural educators than by urban teachers and administrators.
- Getting involved in student disputes was listed by urban and rural educators but not by those in the suburbs.

When asked about their perceived causes for school violence, all three groups, urban, suburban, and rural, listed in their top two (a) a lack of family involvement and supervision with their children/adolescent's lives and (b) the lack of family rules and structure. In responding to questions about ethnicity, 79% of the educators reported the perpetrators were most often White, and 81% indicated that the perpetrators were male. Incidents were perceived to occur primarily at high schools, although the rates of violence in elementary schools and particularly at the middle school level were seen as increasing.

When examined separately, the data on rural schools showed that the rural educators had concerns for their personal safety. They were fearful of verbal and physical threats/attacks from students and from parents and they had experienced some form of violence at least once in the past 2 years.

This study indicates that violent student behaviors are perceived as being a problem in schools, no matter the location. The number of similarities between urban, suburban, and rural districts supports the growing evidence that the gap between urban and rural schools is closing.

A study of rural Texas communities (Kingery et. al., 1990) provides some statistics that more precisely but graphically depict the nature of violence in rural schools. This research showed that in the year prior to the study:

- More than half of the boys and one fifth of the girls engaged in at least one physical fight involving weapons (20% of the boys and 6% of the girls were in three or more such fights).
- One fourth of the students carried a weapon to school.
- Almost 40% of the boys and 8% of the girls carried a knife to school at least once.
- 42% could get a handgun if they wanted to.
- Students frequently engaged in behaviors that placed them at risk for becoming a victim of violence.

Given these figures, neither rural educators nor people living in rural communities can adopt a wait-and-see attitude about school violence. Recognizing and documenting actual occurrences is an important first step toward finding solutions.

Location of Violent Behavior.   In order to curtail violence, teachers and administrators need to know where undesired behavior actually occurs. The answer, according to Hoffman (1996), is as follows:

> Most acts of violence occur where adult supervisor is minimal, or where there are large crowds of people moving to and fro. … violence is more likely to occur in schools where the quality of education is poor.… Most teachers believe that violence occurs in hallways or under staircases, in the lunchroom or cafeteria, or in unattended classrooms. (p. 9)

Students concur but add the gym and locker room as prime sites.

The location of violence differs somewhat in rural schools. When surveyed (Petersen et. al., 1998), rural teachers and administrators reported that violence did not take place primarily in the classroom (classes tend to be small and students are monitored by the teacher), but rather occurred in hallways and restrooms, less often on buses, and at extracurricular/athletic events. In contrast, suburban and urban school personnel indicated that "the classroom was an area of high potential for violence" (p. 27).

School Size.   The emerging interest in school and community violence is renewing the debate over school size. As early as 1977 a study by the New Jersey School Boards Association found that size was the most important predictor of violence in schools. Recent events support this link: "Of the seven recent deadly school shootings in the US, five took place in schools with enrollments close to or over 1,000. They took place in large towns and rural towns, suburbs and cities.... According to the research that's been done, smaller and less crowded schools would appear to be generally safer places" ("Another Take," 1999, p. 2).

Rural schools tend to be small (Hodgkinson, 1994) and so offer the advantage of being less likely than large institutions to attract violent behavior. One explanation is that students in larger schools feel less connected to their teachers and their peers and feel more alienated than students in smaller settings (Warner, Weist, & Krulak, 1999).

The safety advantages of small schools are gaining national attention. The governor of North Carolina, pressing for smaller schools as a means for improving school safety, asserted that small schools provide a forum for more positive attitudes about school, fewer behavior problems, and improved personal relations ("School Size and Violence," 1999). Similarly, the Vermont Department of Education is proposing increased funding for small schools due to the vital role of the school in rural communities ("Vermont Takes Positive Stand," 1999).

School violence does not exist in rural areas to the degree found in larger urban settings, but the problem is growing. An Ohio farmer summarized the rural condition stating, "We are on the same train as city people, but we're in the caboose" (Donnermeyer, 1994, p. 27). More research is needed along with increased alertness on the part of rural citizens. Acknowledging problems of violence is a first step toward exploring solutions, and learning about root sources is the second. Therefore, studies on causes of violence in rural areas are reviewed next.

CAUSES OF RURAL VIOLENCE

One commonly held belief is that crime and violence originate in nearby cities and simply migrate to rural communities, an attitude that places blame on conditions and people elsewhere. Womble and D'Amico (1994) argued that rural areas must look to individual communities for the root causes of increased violence and then identify related solutions. Donnermeyer (1994) pointed to six sets of factors that suggest causal relationships leading to the increase in rural crime rates.

Culture. Traditional rural areas, principally in the southern and western states and in those dominated by mining and timbering, historically have higher rates of violence. Here the use of violence is an accepted means of resolving conflict (Nibsett, 1993).

Poverty. Like many urban neighborhoods, rural areas with persistent poverty over several generations can exhibit higher crime rates. A report undertaken for the Children's Defense Fund (Sherman, 1992) showed that rural children live in poorer families more frequently than do their urban counterparts and school dropout rates are higher than for urban children. An investigation by the U.S. Department of Education (1994) showed that, in 1988, whereas urban youth had the highest rates of risk factors, the number of rural eighth graders having two or more risk factors was significantly higher than those in suburban areas.

Urbanization. Rural areas with higher crime rates are generally (a) located near interstates or large cities and other urban developments, (b) suburbanized (large outer clustering of homes and businesses), (c) locations for second or seasonal homes or other tourist developments, and (d) locations for retired householders moving out of the city.

Rapid Change. Rural areas are increasingly subject to economic and population change that is very rapid. Regardless of whether the change represents an increase or decrease in population, in jobs, or in per-capita income, rapid change can weaken local community norms that reinforce unlawful behavior.

Organized Crime. Some rural areas are the location for organized crime activities, which may include activities ranging from farm equipment or garden tractor theft to drug production. Drug trafficking gangs and their presence can increase crime—especially violent crime.

Urban Export. The movement of urban criminals to rural areas does increase crime. This phenomenon is relatively rare, although it is a common explanation voiced by longtime members of rural communities.

In addition to the six variables cited by Donnermeyer (1994) substance abuse and the availability of guns add to the "deadly mix" that seems to promote violence in rural communities and their schools.

Substance Abuse. The availability and abuse of controlled substances in rural communities and schools have increased dramatically in the past 10 years. Levels appear to approach those reported in urban areas. The following statistics highlight the abuse:

- Use of marijuana and LSD is significantly higher for urban communities but use of smokeless tobacco is higher among rural youth (Donnermeyer, 1994).
- One in five rural males abuse smokeless tobacco on a daily basis.
- The use and abuse of alcohol are similar for urban and rural students (Donnermeyer,1994).
- Rural perpetrators are more likely to be drunk than those in urban areas (Monsey et al., 1995).

Guns.   Nationally, the sale of weapons of deadly force has increased for several years and is reaching all walks of life. Gun control is a serious, politically driven debate and conclusions are far from within our grasp. Regardless of who controls these weapons, they exist in large numbers and are obviously easy for school youth to obtain. Kingery et al. (1990) found that, in rural Texas, 40.8% of the boys and 8.9% of the girls carried a weapon to schools. Some 40% of the boys brought a knife to school at least once, while 19% carried one daily. Slightly more than 6% of the boys brought a handgun to school and 1.6 percent carried a gun daily. Forty-two percent of the students said they could get a handgun if they so desired. Having access to weapons of deadly force does not ensure school violence, but it increases the likelihood. Unfortunately, the mixture of weapons and circumstances, quite often unknown to educators and parents, results in deadly violence.

Prothrow-Stith and Quaday (1996) summed up the complexity of seeking for root causes of violence, whether rural or urban:

> The complex interaction between poverty; racism; drugs and alcohol; the loss of jobs and living wages; gangs, unrestricted and overabundant supplies of guns; lack of personal opportunity and responsibility; disinvestment in communities, schools and after-school activities; family violence and our national admiration of violence plays a critical role in sustaining our culture of violence. (p. 153)

The task of each community is to determine how to address the factors that contribute most to their particular problems and seek appropriate solutions. In rural areas, initiating this task most likely falls to the largest public institution in the community, the school.

DISCUSSION

Our intent is to provide readers with some detail on violence in two different geographic settings, urban and rural. The presentation of this information was offered similarly and in separate sections for urban and rural settings. Here we examine the material first for similarities and differences in violence in the two settings. Second, we offer a brief commentary on how to begin addressing the problems identified.

Probably the most obvious conclusion that can be drawn from the material presented is that in both urban and rural locations the incidents of violence and other crimes are increasing (see Bachman, 1992; Donnermeyer, 1994; Menacker, Weldon, & Horwitz, 1989; Monsey et al., 1995; Portner, 1994; Wright et al., 1992). Additionally, these incidents of violence are pervasive in the lives of those who live in both urban and rural settings. Violence is in schools, on the streets, and in homes. Perhaps most disturbing is the observation that youth violence is one of the most rapidly increasing categories.

Another observation based on the material presented deals with the conditions that appear to contribute to the cause and /or support of violent acts. Some general categories are amazingly similar whether looking at the conditions in rural or urban settings. Generally the influences or factors contributing to or supporting the increase in youth violence seem to sort into three large units: social, economic, and material.

On the social scene, whether in the heart of rural America or in inner-city America, the weakening of traditional social support systems, which come in many forms, has a tremendous influence on fostering an environment in which young people choose behavior that is more violent in nature. Families are less able to provide the traditional social supports due to a variety of factors including divorce, employment at a distance from place of residence, and domestic violence (see Petersen et al., 1998; Stephens, 1994; U.S. Department of Education, 1994). This is true in both rural and urban settings. Social isolation in a variety of forms occurs in both urban and rural settings. Parents working away from their residence leaves them less time to get to know, trust, and depend on others in their neighborhood, and less able to provide supervision of their children's activities. Affiliations with organized religions have generally declined across the country, which has left many young people without a support system of adults and peers with a defined behavioral code.

Poverty reaps damage no matter where it occurs. The earlier information regarding unemployment is alarming. Incidents of violence are much greater where poverty reigns. Being unable to provide basic living requirements induces a level of stress on members of a family that evidences itself in abuse, violence, and theft. Additionally, a lack of opportunity to earn a living through legal means often drives individuals to participate in illegal, and sometimes violent, activities in order to secure basic living requirements.

Material is used here to describe the machines and tools that influence individuals' abilities to perform violent acts. Without a doubt, the most obvious of these is the availability and access to weapons, especially guns. The ease with which youth can secure guns is chilling. Individuals in their early adolescent years have already developed preferred brands of weapons! Another material element that enhances a violence culture is drugs. Again, access and availability have increased in both rural and urban regions. Young people become involved with drugs as users and dealers. Whether defending the trade territory as dealers or securing money to purchase drugs for their own use, youths turn to crimes, including violence, to make this happen.

Finally, after pulling together the resources for this review, it seems obvious that the problem of youth violence is going to require "systems thinking"—viewing contributing factors as being interrelated. Youth violence occurs in every setting and is supported by multiple conditions. Any solutions to youth violence must mirror that context. Offering solutions through schools without any changes in neighborhoods and homes is futile. Likewise, helping raise the economic levels and opportunities of youth and their families is admirable but will be less than effective if students continue to feel isolated and disconnected to their educational institutions.

The causes of school and community violence cannot be confined to one clearly defined set of issues, nor can rural problems be cleanly delineated from those in urban and suburban settings. With regard to school safety in general, Grady (1996) said, "We don't know which problem we are working to solve" (p. 33). The challenge is to determine the relevant problems, find their interrelatedness, identify the antecedents, and, finally, attempt interventions to resolve them. Through collaborative efforts of researchers, educators, parents, and communities of an unprecedented magnitude, to save American's youth, it can and must be done.

CHAPTER ACTIVITIES

For Discussion

1. Consider the quotation by Wilson that introduces this chapter. In small groups discuss its implication for you, your school, your community, and beyond. Attempt to identify some common agreements. Have each small group share their conclusions with the total group.
2. Because the violence problem appears to be nationwide, what role would you want the national, state, and/or local government to play in seeking solutions?
3. The information in the chapter indicates the causes of the violence problem to be multiple and inextricably related. What would you offer as solutions?
4. Consider the multiple conditions that are offered as being causally related to violence. Can they be prioritized—most to least—singularly, in pairs, triads, and so on? How would your answer impact proposed solutions?
5. How does violence in urban, suburban, and rural areas differ—how is it similar? How do responses to violence in the three settings differ? If they do, why?

Case Study

Mr. Allen has been a successful assistant principal at Bowie Middle School for the past 2 years, a school located in the heart of a major urban area. He moved to Honey Grove, a small town an hour's drive from the city to become an assistant principal of a 300-student high school. Mr. Allen is surprised at the relaxed atmosphere of the school and the informal treatment of student problems but is also aware that some students are wearing clothing and accessories similar to that of gangs he dealt with at Bowie. He asked about the need to monitor students for knives, guns, and drugs, but was told, "We don't have that kind of problem here."

Today, two freshmen are in Mr. Allen's office because they were fighting. Mr. Allen suspects the fight is due to a more complicated issue between the boys. Mr. Allen wants to check the boys for weapons, speak with their parents, ask the local police if the boys have been engaged in any criminal activity, and gather information from other students. Sending the boys home for 3 days will make clear his intolerance for violent behavior and allow him time to investigate.

The principal, Mr. Swatsky, disagrees with this approach. He is surprised at the harshness of the punishment and tells Mr. Allen to simply call the boys' homes. He says, "The parents will take care of this. You have to get used to how we do things around here. This is not an inner-city school; these are good kids. You don't understand how upset this community will be if you send a student home for 3 days just because of a fight."

Questions

1. List the key players in this local drama and describe the incident from the perspective of each.
2. What are the critical factors that the administrators need to consider in this situation?
3. Should student misbehavior be dealt with according to community expectations?
4. Was the principal's suggestion too mild? Why?
5. Was Mr. Allen's perspective due to his prior experiences and will that perspective be a help or hindrance in his current job?
6. How could Mr. Allen convince the principal, superintendent, and local community to take gangs and violence more seriously? Outline a detailed plan.
7. If Mr. Swatsky, the principal, were transferred to an inner-city school, what adjustments would he have to make in his approach?

REFERENCES

Another take on school violence. (1999, June). *Rural Policy Matters, 1.4*, 1–2.

Bachman, R. (1992). Crime in non metropolitan America: A national accounting of trends, incidence rates, and idiosyncratic vulnerabilities. *Rural Sociology, 57*(4), 546–560.

Bachus, G. (1994). Twenty-two points, plus triple-word-score, plus fifty points for using all my letters. Game's over. I'm outta here. Violence is no stranger in rural schools. *The School Administrator, 51*(4), 18–22.

Brier, N. (1995). Predicting antisocial behavior in youngsters displaying poor academic achievement: A review at risk factors. *Journal of Developmental and Behavioral Pediatrics, 16*(4), 271–276.

Burrup, P. E., Brimley, V., & Garfield, R. R., (1993). *Financing education in a climate of change* (5th ed.). Needham Heights, MA: Allyn & Bacon.

Center for the Future of Children (1997). *The future of children: Financing schools.* Los Altos, CA: Author.

Donnermeyer, J. F. (1994). Crime and violence in rural communities. In M. Womble & J. D'Amico (Eds.), *Perspectives on violence and substance use in rural America* (pp. 27–64). Oak Brook, IL: North Central Regional Educational Laboratory.

Encyclopedia Britannica Online. (n.d.). Retrieved July 6, 1999 from http// search.eb.com/bol/topic?artcl+111233&seq_mbr+2&samp;page=n& isctn=31&samp;pm=1

Futrell, M. H., & Powell, L. E. (1996). Preventing violence in schools. In W. Schwartz (Ed.), *Preventing youth violence in urban schools: An essay collection* (pp. 1–26). Washington, DC: Office of Educational Research and Improvement.

Gorski, J. D., & Pilotto, L., (1995). Introduction to special issue on violence in educational setting. *Educational Psychology Review, 7*(1), 1–6.

Grady, M. (1996, October). *Rural schools and safety issues.* Paper presented at the annual meeting of the National Rural Education Association, San Antonio, TX.

Green, D. A. (1999). Curbing violence in our public schools: Legal issues dealing with weapons at school. *Insight, 13*(3) 17–20.

Hawkins, D. F. (1996). *Ethnicity, race, class, and adolescent violence* (Center paper 006). Boulder: Center for the Study and Prevention of Violence, University of Colorado.

Hobbs, D. (1994). The rural context for education: Adjusting the images. In M. Womble & J. D'Amico (Eds.), *Perspectives on violence and substance use in rural America* (pp. 5–26). Oak Brook, IL: North Central Regional Educational Laboratory.

Hodgkinson, H. (1999). *The invisible poor: rural youth in America.* Washington, DC: Institute for Educational Leadership.

Huelskamp, R. M. (1993). Perspectives on education in America. *Phi Delta Kappan, 74*(9), 718–721.

Johnson, D. W., & Johnson, R. T. (1995). *Reducing school violence through conflict resolution.* Alexandria, VA: Association for Supervision and Curriculum Development.

Kantor, H., & Brenzel, B. (1993). Urban education and the "truly disadvantaged": The historical roots of the contemporary crisis, 1945–1990. In M. B. Katz (Ed.), *The underclass debate: Views from history* (pp. 366–401). Princeton, NJ: Princeton University press.

Kingery, P., Mirzaee, E., Pruitt, B., & Hurley, R. (1990, Fall). Town and country violence. *School Safety, 22*–25.

Knezevich, S. J. (1984). *Administration of public education: A Sourcebook for the leadership and management of educational institution* (4th ed.). New York: Harper & Row.

Lockwood, A. T. (1993). The wells of violence. *Focus in Change, 10,* 3–6.

McLean, J. E., & Ross, S. M. (1994, October). *The urban–rural funding disparity.* Paper presented at the 86th National Rural Education Association Annual Rural Education Convention, Tuscaloosa, AL.

Menacker, J., Weldon, W., & Hurwitz, E. (1989). School order and safety as community issues. *Phi Delta Kappan, 71*(1), 39–40, 55–56.

Monsey, B., Owen, G., Zierman, C., Lambert, L., & Hyman, V. (1995). *What works in preventing rural violence.* St. Paul, Minnesota: Amherst H. Wilder Foundation.

National Institute of Education. (1978). *Violent schools—Safe schools: The safe school study report to Congress (Executive summary).* Washington, DC: U.S. Department of Health, Education, and Welfare.

National School Boards Association. (1994, January). *Violence in the schools.* Alexandria, VA: Author.

Nisbett, R. E. (1993). Violence and U.S. regional culture. *The American Psychologist, 48,* 441–449.

Petersen, G. J., Beekley, C. Z., Speaker, K. M., & Pietrzak, D. (1998). An examination of violence in three rural school districts. *Journal for Rural and Small Schools,19*(3), 25–38.

Portner, J. (1994, January 12). School violence up over past 5 years, 82% in survey say. *Education Week,* p. 9.

Prothrow-Stith, D. (1994). Violence: Building prevention into the curriculum. *The School Administrator, 51*(4), 8–12.

Prothrow-Stith, D. B. (1995). The epidemic of youth violence in America: Using public health prevention strategies to prevent violence. *Journal of Health Care for the Poor and Underserved, 6*(2), 95–101.

Prothrow-Stith, D., & Quaday, S. (1996). Communities, schools, and violence. In A. M. Hoffman (Ed.), *Schools, violence. and society* (pp. 153–161). Westport, CT: Praeger.

Riester, A. E., & Deegear, J. (1997). Urban youth gangs: Ecological intervention strategies. In N. K. Phillips & L. A. Straussner (Eds.), *Children in the urban environment—Linking social policy and clinical practice* (pp. 78–90). Springfield, IL: Thomas.

School size and violence. (1999, September). *Rural Policy Matters, 1.7,* 1–2.

Sherman, A. (1992). *Falling by the wayside: Children in rural America.* Washington, DC: Children's Defense Fund.

Simmons, W. (1999). *The changing face of education: Urban schools in the new millennium.* Paper presented at the symposium on race relations sponsored by The Center for the Study of Race and Ethnicity in America, Providence, RI.

Stephens, R. D. (1994, January). Gangs, guns and school violence. *USA Today, 122*(2584), 29–32.

Stern, J. D. (1992). How demographic trends for the eighties affect rural and small-town schools. *Educational Horizons, 70*(2), 71–77.

Sukkoo, I. (2000). Urban development in the United States, 1690–1990. *Southern Economic Journal, 66*(4), 855–880.

Takata, S. R. (1994). A community comparison of "youth gang" prevention strategies. In *Perspectives on violence and substance use in rural American* (pp. 95–124). Oakbrook, IL: Midwest Regional Center for Drug-Free Schools and Communities and the North Central Regional Educational Laboratory.

U.S. Census Bureau. (1991). *Comparison summary measures of income by selected characteristics.* Washington, DC: U.S. Government Printing Office.

U.S. Census Bureau. (1996). *Comparison summary measures of income by selected characteristics.* Washington, DC: U.S. Government Printing Office.

U.S. Census Bureau. (1997). *Comparison summary measures of income by selected characteristics.* Washington, DC: U.S. Government Printing Office.

U.S. Department of Education, Office of Educational Research and Improvement. (1994). *The condition of education in rural schools.* Washington, DC: U.S. Government Printing Office.

Vermont takes positive stand on schools (1999, April). *Rural Policy Matters, 1.2,* 1–2.

Vocational Foundation, Inc. (1978). *Our turn to listen: A white paper on unemployment, education and crime based on extensive interviews with New York City teenage dropouts.* New York: Author. (ERIC Document Reproduction Service No. ED152871).

Warner, B., Weist, M., & Krulak, A. (1999). Risk factors for school. *Urban Education, 34*(1), 52–68.

Wilson, J. Q. (1993). *Thinking about crime.* New York: Vintage Books.

Womble, M., & D'Amico, J. J. (Eds.). (1994). *Perspectives on violence and substance use in rural America.* Oak Brook, IL: North Central Regional Educational Laboratory.

World Book Multimedia Encyclopedia. (1999). Chicago: World Book, Inc.

Wright, J. D., Sheley, J. F., & Smith, M. D. (1992). Kids, guns, and killing fields. *Society, 30,* 84–89.

Youth violence: Gangs on Main Street, USA. (1997). *Issues in Brief* (A report from the Pew Partnership for Civil Change Program). Philadelphia: Pew Charitable Trusts.

3

Decreasing School Violence: A Research Synthesis

Carolyn Kneese
Harry Fullwood
Gwen Schroth
Anita Pankake
Texas A&M University-Commerce

In the foreword to *Saving Our Children*, Heymann (1996) asserted that the world of violence has changed very little since the 1970s but identified as new the "burst of youth violence" (p. 8). Similarly, Hawkins (1996) stated, "Since the mid-1980s acts of interpersonal violence committed by and against adolescents have symbolized the crime problem in the United States and have been said to pose a major threat to the public's health and safety" (p. 1). The increase in juvenile crime includes acts that were described as unthinkable in the recent past but now commonplace. Such incidents as drive-by shootings, gang warfare, in-school shootings, and so on, are still shocking but less surprising (Wright, Sheley, & Smith, 1992). Prothrow-Stith (1995) described the situation as "an epidemic of youth violence" (p. 96).

As a result of this "epidemic," the literature on solutions to student-related crime and violence in schools takes on new meaning for educators as well as the public. In this chapter we seek to review that literature and attempt to bring some order to the variety of answers professionals have put forth for educators, students, parents, and communities. For this purpose some 24 books, 45 journal articles, and 17 papers and reports primarily from educational sources were examined. To search out patterns or major themes in the literature, each recommended solution was carefully analyzed. The following three themes emerged and are addressed in turn: solutions for which adults have primary responsibility, those that place more burden on students, and those that call for involving the larger school community.

WHAT ADULTS CAN DO ABOUT SCHOOL VIOLENCE

Most of the literature on school-related solutions to youth violence and crime is directed at adult caretakers and, understandably, most literature written for educators addresses activities in which teachers and administrators take the lead. A small number of solutions to school violence are directed at the primary caregivers, the parents.

School Personnel: Teachers and Administrators

Interventions suggested for teachers and administrators sort readily into four categories: providing education and training, creating a caring climate, controlling student behavior, and changing physical/structural arrangements.

Education and Training. The most frequently cited prevention measure recommended for adults is education and training of teachers, staff, and administrators (Dusenbury, Falco, Lake, Branningan, & Bosworth, 1997; Futrell & Powell, 1996; Guerra, Tolan, & Hammond, 1996; Johnson & Johnson, 1995). In some instances this training should include students (Johnson & Johnson, 1995; Petersen, Beekley, Speaker, & Pietrzak, 1998). Training and education cover a broad span of approaches and address an array of risk factors for aggression. Most frequently they try to promote prosocial behavior through psycho-educational programming directed at children and their teachers, schools, peers, or families. Guerra et al. (1996) suggested that bolstering prosocial competencies should relate to reductions in antisocial and aggressive behavior. Gorski and Pilotto (1995) proposed that these prevention models be integrated in every school's curricula allowing students to relate and connect the learning to their present realities in meaningful ways. Dusenbury et al. (1997) advised that interventions begin in the early grades, be developmentally appropriate, and include interactive techniques.

Among the models most frequently cited is social-skills training for teachers and students. Cartledge (1996) offered guidelines for improving social behaviors of aggressive students. She also included strategies for bridging gaps between children from diverse cultures. In a comparison of violence in urban, suburban, and rural schools, Petersen et al. (1998) found that "While nine of the ten most commonly implemented programs were similar, one strategy was unique to the rural schools ... the use of social skills training of teachers and students" (p. 29). Interestingly, all three groups, rural, suburban, and urban educators, listed addressing poverty issues as their most frequently used strategy.

Conflict resolution and mediation facilitation are other commonly cited training models. These constitute teaching self-regulatory skills, promoting metacognitive strategies for self-prevention of aggressive acts, and include direct instruction of morals and ethical values (Lantieri, DeJong, & Dutrey, 1996). Such models are based on the belief that people should listen to one another when a problem arises and work toward a peaceful solution.

The advantage of training programs is that they can be incorporated into the regular curriculum and/or delivered by a local police officer. One example of such a program is the Gang Resistance Education and Training (GREAT) program where police officers spend time in classrooms discussing problems of drugs, gangs, and other issues linked to juvenile offenses. Concurrently, they teach students how to resolve conflicts and make appropriate decisions. The goal is to decrease the popularity of gangs and prevent, suppress, and intervene in other juvenile offenses. The success of this program is attributed to the dedication and commitment of the police officers who work in the schools and the interest of the recipients, including gang members (Huff & Trump, 1996).

Creating a Caring Climate.   Another approach to preventing violent student behavior is altering the school environment by developing healthy relationships between adults and students. Katz, Noddings, and Strike (1999) advocated creating schools where students feel cared for and safe. Posner (1994) pointed out that children at high risk of violence, academic failure, drug abuse, and dropping out of schools often lack a connection to a positive social entity, such as a family, peer group, or church. Sergiovanni (1995) described a study in which researchers examined four culturally diverse schools and concluded, "Participants feel the crisis inside schools is directly linked to human relationships. Most often mentioned were relationships between teachers and students. Where positive things about the schools are noted, they usually involve reports of individuals who care, listen, understand, respect others, and are honest, open and sensitive" (p. 70). Sapphire (1999) advocated reconnecting with youth saying, "The public in public schools must insist on redefinition and institutional change. The public must insist that all students, congruent with and integral to their education, will truly be known within their schools" (p. 5), although Sapphire admitted this will not guarantee violence will end. Friedland (1999), referencing the anger and alienation generated in schools as they are currently configured, suggested putting into place purposeful programs that make the culture of the school community friendlier, less threatening, and far more rewarding.

Relationships among students and between teachers and students can be strengthened. Studies point to a variety of effective methods for doing so. Ethiel (1996) found that conducting class meetings increased opportunities for teachers to interact with students; Friedland (1999) encouraged the use of cooperative learning strategies to increase student-to-student exchanges. Featherstone advocated reducing school size and creating schools-within-a-school as early as 1987 for similar purposes.

Johnson and Johnson (1995) pointed out that conflict, particular when due to bias and discrimination, interferes with constructive relationships. Strategies provided by Cartledge and Milburn (1995) are helpful in reducing bias and conflict between students. Some tactics are specifically directed at problems that arise when students are from diverse backgrounds. Wubbles (1992) suggested that assessing teachers' interpersonal skills may be an important first step toward improving classroom relationships.

Studies on school climate show positive results when healthy relationships are formed among students and between students and their teachers. Care and concern, though, are nearly impossible to monitor, difficult to measure, and challenging for secondary teachers to execute when they interact with 175–200 students each day.

Closing the Gaps.   Tightening the school's grip on student behavior is frequently mentioned in the literature as a method for reducing antisocial behavior. Some advice specifically for teachers follows:

- Leave classroom doors open. As a classroom situation develops, a passing teacher or student can alert someone for assistance (Bender & McLaughlin, 1997).
- Monitor hallways. Petersen et al. (1998) found that educators in rural, suburban, and urban schools ranked placing teachers in hallways as one of their most effective violence prevention strategies.
- Respond to student rumors. Rumors of potential violence or weapons violations, along with the estimated seriousness of those rumors, should be reported to the principal (Bender & McLaughlin, 1997).
- Form a buddy system in which each teacher is paired with the teacher across the hall. The paired teachers routinely check with each other after class starts to ensure things are going smoothly (Bender & McLaughlin, 1997).
- Be cognizant of the whereabouts of students who have been violent before. Notice if they are in a location where they are not usually present (Bender & McLaughlin, 1997).
- Discuss school crisis intervention plans with all staff and volunteers so they are ready to act when an event occurs (Walker & Gresham, 1997).
- Maintain a zero tolerance for weapons and any acts of violence (Stephens, 1995). Students are well aware of what is tolerated and what is not and act accordingly.

Additionally, Walker and Gresham (1997) advocated tightening the grip on student academic behavior as well by increasing performance expectations for all students in order to combat unwanted student behavior.

Physical/Structural Changes. Some preventive measures involve changing tangible arrangements in the school. Some changes are simple whereas others involve long-range planning and considerable expense. Suggestions are to:

- Remove lockers (Petersen et al., 1998; Poland, 1999). Lockers are convenient hiding places for guns and drugs. Additionally, student conflict commonly occurs in hallways (Hoffman & Summers, 1996) so removing lockers reduces the amount of time students spend in the halls. Altering bell schedules so that all students are not in the halls at the same time and requiring hall passes during class time can also reduce students' opportunities for hallway conflict.
- Close campuses and institute before- and after-school programs (Petersen et al., 1998). Closing the campus and instituting programs outside of regular school hours increases the number of opportunities to supervise students.
- Minimize the number of unlocked entrances (Stephens, 1995). Some violent acts are perpetrated on students by people outside the school. Installing doors that are locked from the outside but not from within, allowing easy exit in case of emergencies, can reduce access to the building.
- Improve avenues for communication by installing surveillance cameras, private phone lines, fax machines, cell phones, metal detectors, and two-way radios (Poland, 1999). In crisis situations, communication may make the difference between a controllable situation and a full-blown emergency.

District long-range plans should include safety features. Suggestions are to:

- Design or modify physical facilities to that they can be easily supervised (Walker, Irvin, & Sprague, 1997). Spaces hidden from view provide ready opportunities for drug transactions and sexual misconduct.
- Reduce school size (Featherstone, 1987). "Of seven recent deadly school shootings in the United States, five took place in schools with enrollments close to or over 1,000 students" ("Another Take on School Violence," 1999, p. 1). Smaller and less crowded schools appear to be safer places.

Altering physical arrangements alone will not prevent violence although, when implemented in conjunction with other measures, do support the staff's efforts and make students aware that safety is everywhere and always a priority.

Additional Interventions.   Johnson and Johnson (1995) emphasized the need for teachers and students to learn to cope with violent student behaviors as they occur. Most administrators develop crisis management plans written for and by teachers to fit the school's unique circumstances. Whatever measures are planned, Beyer (1996) cautioned that such plans include only actions condoned by the court. Beyer suggested that interventions include more than direct and radical measures such as car searches, metal detectors, urine analyses, and drug-sniffing dogs, actions more often perceived as effective by urban and suburban educators (Petersen et al., 1998).

Bender and McLaughlin (1997) and Poland (1999) offered specific but sobering advice for managing nonthreatening weapons violations, hostage situations, and explosive situations that occur on campus where someone with a weapon begins firing:

- Verify facts so that actions taken will be appropriate and efficient.
- Nonconfrontationally isolate the student who nonthreateningly produces a weapon. Also remove other students from the site.
- Avoid heroics such as lunging for a gun. Rather, keep a safe distance, keep hands visible, and avoid abrupt movements.
- Look for a place to dive or jump when managing a hostage situation. Negotiations may not always be effective so think about an escape plan for yourself and others.

Administrators have some specific responsibilities during a hostage crisis. These should be planned in advance and shared with the staff:

- Use code words for firearms when engaging in radio communications and alerting teachers over the PA (public address) system.
- Close blinds in empty classrooms and rooms where the crisis is not occurring so that a perpetrator outside the building cannot see potential victims.
- Teach teachers and students to take cover away from windows when a crisis occurs.
- Be prepared to deal immediately with police and medical personnel, the media, and parents.

The advantage of developing crisis plans is that they can be tailored to each school's setting and needs. Staff training on the plan helps ensure that everyone responds appropriately and that the crisis is dealt with efficiently.

Nonschool Personnel: Parents

Some scholars place particularly strong emphasis on the role of the home in student behavior. "Such a perspective is supported by an accumulating literature that suggests that family variables are important in the development and treatment of antisocial and violent behavior" (Guerra et al., 1996, p. 393). Tolan, Guerra, and Kendall (1995) stated that "Among the individual risk factors for antisocial behavior, there is convergent evidence supporting the influence of social-cognitive factors, and these factors are viable foci for intervention. Similarly, there is growing consistency of evidence of parenting and family relation risk influences and efficacy as intervention targets" (p. 581). Not surprising then is Davis' (1994) conclusion that interventions with violent youth cannot be isolated from interventions with family systems.

Many factors associated with youth violence are related to home and family (Petersen et al., 1998; Poland, 1999). Many involve actions that parents do—or fail to do—with and to their children and for which parents can and should take responsibility. These include:

- Child abuse.
- Ineffective parenting.
- Violence acted out by parents or tolerated in the home.
- Lack of family involvement/supervision with children's/adolescent's lives.
- Lack of family rules/structure.
- Parental drug abuse.
- Lack of family involvement in moral/religious activities.
- Violence viewed on television.

Poverty is also associated with youth violence, a condition over which parents may have less control. Society as a whole must take an interest.

Frequently mentioned in the literature is the need to increase parent involvement in schools. Including parents as partners has the advantage of providing broader support for school concerns. Also, the presence of parents at school and school-related activities can help reduce students' worries about violence (Cooledge et al., 1995).

On the other hand, all too familiar to educators are the parents who, for whatever reason, do not involve themselves in their children's schools. The challenge for schools is to find avenues for connecting with these parents. Also familiar to educators are the parents who are loud, argumentative, and even violent on school grounds and who thus become the problem.

The literature provides suggestions for developing healthy parental involvement in schools. Advice is to:

- Enlist their aid in creating crisis intervention plans (Walker & Gresham, 1997).
- Include family members in programs targeting youth and high-risk young adults (Monsey, Owen, Qierman, Lambert, & Hyman, 1995).
- Make frequent home visits (Burstyn & Stevens, 1999). These visits allow parents to learn that the teacher or administrator cares about their child. Additionally, communication between the school and parents is increased, and the educators are likely to understand better the child's emotional and physical background.
- Conduct parent-training sessions to bring caretakers closer to the school's concerns (Futrell & Powell, 1996; Johnson & Johnson, 1995). Parent and community volunteers are often invaluable to the operation of the school. Volunteers are cited as being particularly helpful when it comes to preventing school violence.
- Improve safety by simply increasing the number of adults in the school building (Poland, 1999).
- Aid in monitoring school halls, entrances, and exits (Walker & Gresham, 1997).
- Take formal and informal actions to communicate student behavior and dress codes (Walker & Gresham, 1997).

During a violent situation at school, Bender and McLaughlin (1997) suggested contacting a parent if the student agrees. They cautioned, though, that administrators should use code words in radio communications because parents may be monitoring the police channel, become alarmed, and flood the school with calls or with their presence. After a crisis, follow-up activities with the family and others directly involved are important. Families need to debrief and may even profit from counseling. Teachers and students need opportunities to share their fears and concerns. School counselors are particularly helpful at this juncture.

STUDENT INVOLVEMENT IN VIOLENCE PREVENTION

Educational systems are faced with a myriad of interpersonal problems and conflicts between students. "The majority of students enter school wanting to learn. They become at-risk for failure within America's schools as a result of a variety of conditions over which they often do not have any control" (Dorrell, 1993, p. 11). Students have no control over the size of the school, the teachers who are hired, or the homes from which they come. They do have some control over the decision to stay in school, the friends they choose, the behavior and attitudes they adopt, and even have some collective power to influence their school's environment. Yet all too often programs are designed around what adults can enact or do together with students rather than planned around what students, themselves, find worthy of their commitment. The need to involve those for whom programs are designed is highlighted by Bourgeois' (1996) example of the failure of Johnson's War on Poverty that "came from the top and left out of the decision making process the most important constituency: the people it was designed to help" (p. 309).

Some violence prevention strategies do stress student involvement. Many are directed at skill building. Following are some examples:

- Social-skills and competency training, which require students to take the initiative to change their own behavior.
- Training that requires and assesses changes in students' attitudes and beliefs.
- Self-esteem and negotiating-skills training, which empower students to take charge of their own lives.
- Interactive techniques such as peer mediation and/or conflict resolution.

One administrator who shared her power and control by involving teachers in the school's everyday decision making greatly increased teacher morale (Schroth & Dunbar, 1993). Might sharing decision-making responsibilities with students also change how they feel about and behave in school?

Changing Behavior, Attitudes, and Beliefs

Involving students in violence prevention strategies touches the surface of what is needed. At a deeper level is the need to impact students' behavior, attitudes, and beliefs. Illustrative activities for reaching those students at risk for violence include:

- Cognitive behavior modification and social-skills training (Dahlberg, 1998).
- Social learning theory and anger replacement therapy (Dusenbury et al., 1997).
- Education to develop "street smarts," which can help students to deal with violence in their own lives (Kirby, 1995; Trotter, 1993).
- Instruction on other students' cultural backgrounds to improve interpersonal relationships (Cartledge, 1996).

A major advantage of education and training programs is that individual students do not have to be identified as being prone to violent behavior to receive the benefits of such interventions. On the other hand, these social competence programs typically consist of a uniform intervention offered to all individuals (who may or may not choose to participate) and are not sensitive to differences in need (Guerra et al., 1996) or cultural variations:

It is naive to expect that all teenagers will respond equally to the same intervention and need the same type and level of services. In particular, it is unlikely that youth who have progressed from childhood aggression to more
serious and habitual adolescent violence will respond to broad-based educational or social development programs. (Guerra et al., 1996, p. 386).

On a more positive note, conducting such programs during the preschool
years may generate reductions in aggression that last into adolescence
(Zigler, Taussig, & Black, 1992).

Moving Students Toward Adulthood

Educating children includes helping them become responsible and mature
adults. Some educators emphasize increasing student empowerment
through inclusionary schoolwide management practices. Baker (1998) suggested that giving youth a legitimate "voice" in the school community
should result in preventing violence. School-based peer mediation and
conflict resolution programs are techniques that focus on peer-group interactions and empower students to help one another. Though less common
than individual approaches, programs such as peer mediation are now
more frequently found in schools (Close & Lechman, 1997; Dahlberg, 1998).
The advantages of peer mediation and conflict resolution programs is that
students deal with conflicts without adult assistance and learn how to positively state what they need to resolve their problems. Thus they are better
equipped for adult life (Bickmore, 1993; Cueto, Bosworth, & Sailes, 1993;
Hakim, 1992; Jacobson & Lombard, 1992; Maxwell, 1989; Schomberg, 1992).

Creating conditions that help students become responsible citizens is a
priority for educators. Yet not all students take advantage of or are given
such opportunities. A pertinent question is whether or not the students
who most need help are actually included in the intervention programs,
and, if not, what can the staff and students do to reach them? Concurrently,
while students work to become more responsible citizens, so must the staff.
Yet too many adults in schools do not settle their own problems (Burstyn &
Stevens, 1999), modeling the very behavior students are told not to exhibit.

Changing the Environment

In contrast to interventions that emphasize skill-building techniques, some
programs seek to modify environmental influences on youth behavior. Students' attitudes, beliefs, and behavior are expected to change when the settings that young people inhabit on a daily basis are altered. William DeJong
(1994), lecturer at the Harvard School of Public Health, said, "The best
school-based violence prevention programs seek to do more than reach the
individual child. They instead try to change the total school environment, to
create a safe community that lives by a credo of non-violence and multicul-

tural appreciation" (p. 8), all of which require student involvement for success. Some examples of student-initiated environmental changes follow:

- Student adoption of school uniforms.
- Drug-free programs such as Drug Free Youth in Texas (DFYIT), a program in which students voluntarily undergo drug testing.
- Student assessment of the safety of the school setting. The National School Safety Center has developed the School Crime Assessment Tools for school. It recommends enlisting student leaders to communicate desired student behavior (Stephens, 1995).

Embry (1997) advocated creating a climate of change so that school is a peaceful and nurturing environment. An example of a program that calls for student initiative in creating a positive climate is Peace Builders, applied successfully in numerous schools across the nation. In this program all persons in the school community are asked to commit to a common language reinforced by positive peer pressure to maintain certain standards of behavior.

Student-initiated interventions, particularly those in which students help one another, tap into students' need for acceptance and belonging and take advantage of the fact that school is a social domain in which peer associations exert considerable influence on youth behavior (Sommers & Baskin, 1994). Success is limited to the strength student leaders exhibit in initiating and implementing the interventions.

EXTERNAL ENTITIES: INVOLVING THE COMMUNITY

School violence is too complex for any one professional group or institution to solve. Guerra et al. (1996) argued that, although the school may reduce the occurrence of violent acts in schools, their effects are unlikely to generalize to other settings or discourage an individual's propensity to engage in violent acts. Dusenbury et al. (1997) and Bemak and Keys (2000) suggested that partnerships among schools, communities, and families are required for violence to be reduced. The literature offers a wide variety of suggestions for communities to fulfill their responsibility to such partnerships.

Programs and Aid

Some community-wide efforts are aimed at creating prevention programs and providing assistance to victims of crime and violence. Monsey and others (1995) suggested that communities first conduct a needs assessment to determine their most pressing problems and then determine community goals. A variety of interventions are then possible. Communities can create crisis counseling centers, build safe houses, provide tutoring and conflict mediation for local students and their parents, institute drug-counseling programs, and arrange recreation and arts for families and neighborhoods (Futrell & Powell, 1996; Monsey et al., 1995).

Communities can also target school dropouts and expelled students for interventions. Local organizations can create jobs, organize on-the-job training, and provide employment counseling to prevent these youth from engaging in criminal activity (Vocational Foundations, 1978). Poland (1999) suggested that communities can cooperate with schools to institute reentry programs for students expelled from school. Guerra et al. (1996) recommended that these diversionary programs target juveniles identified by the justice system and Hoffman and Summers (1996) recommended gang members for inclusion as well.

Ultimately, all community-based efforts need to be networked and coordinated (Cooledge et al., 1995). Individual programs are not as effective as the combined efforts of an entire community. In arguing for cooperative, comprehensive solutions on the part of education, employment, and health care agencies, Hamner (1993) quoted one Kansas state legislator as saying, "One more government program, one more cop on the street is not going to work. The community needs to take responsibility and initiative that develop at the grass roots level to reclaim the neighborhood and intervene in the lives of its youth. We need a whole neighborhood philosophy. No single approach works" (p. 5).

Tighter Controls

Some schools, particularly those in urban and suburban areas, institute direct and radical measures such as metal detectors to prevent violence (Petersen et al., 1998). Community groups and law enforcement agencies, likewise, can tighten direct controls. Suggestions in the literature are to:

- Form organized street patrols (Monsey et al., 1995).
- Institute firearms restrictions (Monsey et al., 1995).
- Place police in schools (Phillips, 1997) so students who behave violently or violate the law can be arrested (Johnson & Johnson, 1995).
- Involve police in planning response procedures for school crisis situations (Bachus, 1994).
- Reestablish the balance of rewards and penalties in the juvenile justice system (Vocational Foundations, 1978).
- Increase legislative support such as that provided by The Safe Schools Act of 1993 (Bourgeois, 1996) and increase legislated penalties that treat schools like airports so threats will be taken seriously (Poland, 1999).

Again, collaboration is essential for interventions to be effective. An example of school–community collaboration described by Cortines (1996) is an ambitious series of initiatives undertaken by the New York City School

Board. They instituted (a) community policing (becoming familiar with patterns of crime and places and situations that create the opportunity for crimes to be committed, knowing the ins and outs of a neighborhood, forging partnerships between enforcement services and clients), (b) School Safety Zones created in cooperation with the New York City Police Department, which resulted in increased safety coverage of school entrances, major city corridors to the schools, train stations and bus stops, (c) neighborhood clusters of schools with similar problems for the purpose of coordinating safety measures, and (d) boroughwide advisory councils to establish 24-hour hotlines and cosponsor after-school athletic leagues where School Safety Officers participate as coaches and referees.

Parents and Families

A word about parents and families in particular is appropriate here. Although a significant number of factors connected with school violence stem from the home, the literature reviewed here targeted schools for prevention and intervention. Some researchers stress that for comprehensive, multifaceted collaboration schools need to include families. Though engaging families in school activities is not always an easy task, some suggestions for engaging families in prevention measures are to provide:

- Education and training with the goal of teaching parents to effectively discipline, monitor, and supervise youth (Dahlberg, 1998).
- School–family community health teams (Bemak & Keys, 2000).
- Before- and after-school programs for youth (Petersen et al., 1998).

Monsey and others (1995) examined a number of strategies to reduce violence. Among those that were rated "effective" or "moderately effective" and that involved parents and families were:

- Police and citizen intervention teams.
- Safe houses or shelters.
- Mental health services.
- Crisis hotlines.
- Spouse abuse treatment programs.
- Comprehensive home visits.
- Foster care for abused children.
- Therapeutic day care and therapeutic support for families.
- Juvenile and adult sex offender treatment programs.

Interventions that primarily target the home and family are often most difficult to carry out because family violence is often hidden and because solutions call for invading privacy and individual rights. Nevertheless, creating services for families and making them available through community organizations as well as through schools does provide opportunities of which children and adults can take advantage should they choose.

CONCLUSION

A substantial body of research surrounding youth violence and crime is available to educators. Suggested solutions for schools to implement are in abundance. The most effective remedies involve collaborative efforts of school, home, students, as well as the community. After reviewing the literature on prevention measures for school violence, Futrell and Powell (1996) concluded that it is important for communities to urge all local groups and individuals to work with schools to ensure implementation of comprehensive and long-term strategies to support successful youth development. It stands to reason that students who feel strongly connected to all three, their family, their community, and their school, are at lower risk for violence.

To accomplish such connections, adults within and outside the schools must first acknowledge that in 5 to 10 years today's youth will soon become part of the adult population. Within 5 to 10 years, these young people will be expected to safeguard and enhance the civil, human, political, and economic rights of the citizens of our country and it is the future of this nation and the kind of society we want that is at stake (Futrell & Powell, 1996).

Second, adults within and outside schools must take the time and make the effort to collaboratively review their community's unique needs and adopt those alternatives that will create healthy environments that will aid and encourage students themselves to make proper choices. Futrell and Powell (1996) speculated about appropriating for community use the thousands of dollars spent on such measures as metal detectors and security guards each year but that have not eliminated school violence or made students or staff feel safer:

> What would happen if some of those dollars were used to create jobs for youth, build recreation facilities for children, establish year-round counseling and tutoring programs for students who need them? What would happen if child care programs were established in schools so children could receive supervised attention, rather than stay at home alone for hours? What would happen if instead of sending adolescents to boot camp, we sent them to residential academies where they could learn about math, science, computers, and have fun at the same time? What would happen if more of these children were in programs like Outward Bound? These types of investments would yield far more for our tax dollars and be more beneficial to society than installing metal detectors in school or hiring more hall monitors. (p. 6)

Whatever the interventions, adults can and must improve the environments that students call "my home," "my school," "my neighborhood," and "my community." Then, and only then, will the "epidemic of youth violence," like some other social ills, become manageable.

CHAPTER ACTIVITIES

For Discussion

1. Make a list of the violence and crime incidents in your school during the past 6 months. Group these into larger categories (theft, fights, verbal threats, etc.). Finally, match appropriate prevention strategies suggested in this chapter to those categories. Keep in mind the expectations of the larger school community.

2. Can educators realistically expect students to become involved in violence prevention in their schools? If so, how would you raise student interest in such an endeavor?

3. Are there drawbacks to having parents highly involved in schools? If so, what are they and how can they be overcome?

4. Create a list of ways in which parents can be persuaded to become more involved in your school.

Case Study

Pine Middle School is located in a suburb of a large city and has an enrollment of about 800 students. The school has recently experienced a number of incidents that are disturbing to the teachers and the principal. Ten students are wearing gang-related hats and scarves. During the past 6 weeks, three fights disrupted passing periods and two were found to be a result of disagreements between students suspected of being gang members. At yesterday's faculty meeting teachers complained to the principal, Mr. Stahl, that students were increasingly using vulgar language toward each other and beginning to openly display rude behavior toward teachers. The staff wants to know what is being done about the fights and asks Mr. Stahl to clarify which type of verbal behavior warrants sending a student to the office for discipline.

Today the English Department is meeting to address curriculum issues but the Team Leader, Mrs. Thompson, cannot begin the meeting because the six English teachers are talking heatedly about the increase in student misbehavior. The teachers express concern that allowing disrespectful behavior to continue will ultimately contribute to the type of violent outbursts they hear is occurring in a neighboring suburb. Mrs. Thompson does not know whether to make student behavior the agenda issue or to insist that the Team return to the curriculum decisions that need to be made.

Questions.

1. What are the major issues about which Mr. Stahl, the principal, should be concerned?
2. Can one team of teachers bring about change that involves the larger school community? If not, who should take responsibility for initiating change?
3. What information would you need to have to design a plan for improving student behavior at Pine Middle School?
4. Of the solutions offered in this chapter, which might be appropriate for Pine Middle School?
5. How similar are the problems in this school to those in your school?
6. Should Mrs. Thompson allow the Team to continue discussing student behavior or should she bring them back to the curriculum issues? Why?

REFERENCES

Another take on school violence. (1999, June). *Rural Policy Matters,* pp. 1–2.

Bachus, G. (1994). Violence is no stranger in rural schools. *School Administrator, 51*(4), 18–22.

Baker, J. A. (1998). Are we missing the forest for the trees? Considering the social context of school violence. *Journal of School Psychology, 36*(1), 29–44.

Bemak, F., & Keys, S. (2000). *Violent and aggressive youth: Intervention and prevention strategies for changing times.* Thousand Oaks, CA: Corwin Press.

Bender, W. N., & McLaughlin, P. J. (1997, March). Weapons violence in schools: Strategies for teachers confronting violence and hostage situations. *Intervention in School and Clinic, 32*(4), 211–216.

Beyer, D. (1996). School violence and the legal rights of students: Selected issues. In W. Schwartz (Ed.), *Preventing youth violence in urban schools: An essay collection* (pp. 55–79). Washington, DC: Office of Educational Research and Improvement.

Bickmore, K. (1993). Peer mediation: Conflict resolution in schools. *Journal of School Psychology, 31*, 427–430.

Bourgeois, C. (1996). Violence in schools: The Texas initiative. In A. M. Hoffman (Ed.), *Schools, violence, and society* (pp. 297–317). Westport, CT: Praeger.

Burstyn, J. N., & Stevens, R. (1999, April). *Education in conflict resolution: Creating a whole school approach.* Paper presented at the American Educational Research Association Conference, Montreal, Canada.

Cartledge, G. (1996). *Cultural diversity and social skills instruction.* Champaign, IL: Research Press.

Cartledge, G., & Milburn, J. (1995). *Teaching social skills to children and youth.* Needham Heights, MA: Allyn & Bacon.

Close, C. L., & Lechman, K. (1997). Fostering youth leadership: Students train students and adults in conflict resolution. *Theory Into Practice, 36*(1), 11–16.

Cooledge, N. J., Barrons, M. F., Coine, L. N., Geller, P., Keeney, V., Meier, R. D., & Paul, D. M. (1995, May). Are their worlds and worries different? *Schools in the Middle,* pp. 34–37.

Cortines, R. C. (1996). The New York City Board of Education and violence prevention. In A. M. Hoffman (Ed.), *Schools, violence, and society* (pp. 265–273). Westport, CT: Praeger.

Cueto, S., Bosworth, K., & Sailes, J. (1993, April). *Promoting peace: Integrating curricula to deal with violence.* Paper presented at the annual meeting of the American Educational Research Association, Atlanta, GA.

Dahlberg, L. (1998). Youth violence in the United States: Major trends, risk factors, and prevention approaches. *American Journal of Preventive Medicine, 14*(4), 259–272.

Davis, E. (1994, November). Youth violence and the changing family. A study of family background factors. In *Published proceedings of the First National Conference on Urban Issues* (pp. 200–242). Buffalo: State University of New York College at Buffalo.

DeJong, W. (1994). School-based violence preventions: From the peaceable school to the peaceable neighborhood. *Forum, 25, 8.*

Dorrell, L. D. (1993, October). *You can't look forward to tomorrow, while holding on to yesterday: Rural education and the at-risk student.* Paper presented at the Annual Conference of National Rural Education Association, Burlington, VT.

Dusenbury, L., Falco, M., Lake, A., Brannigan, R., & Bosworth, K. (1997). Nine critical elements of promising violence prevention programs. *Journal of School Health, 67*(10), 409–414.

Embry, D. D. (1997, March). Does your school have a peaceful environment? Using an audit to create a climate for change and resiliency. *Intervention in School and Clinic, 32*(4), 217–222.

Ethiel, N. (1996). *Saving our children: Can youth violence be prevented?* (Published proceedings of the Harvard Law School Center for Criminal Justice Interdisciplinary Conference). Cambridge, MA: Harvard Law School.

Featherstone, H. (1987). Orderly classrooms and corridors: Why some schools have them and others don't. *The Harvard Education Letter, III,* (5), 1–5.

Friedland, S. (1999). Less violence? Change school culture. *The Education Digest, 65*(1), 6–9.

Futrell, M. J., & Powell, L. E. (1996). Preventing violence in schools. In W. Schwarz (Ed.), *Preventing youth violence in urban schools: An essay collection* (pp. 1–26). Washington, D.C.: Office of Educational Research and Improvement.

Gorski, J. D., & Pilotto, L. (1995). Introduction to special issue on violence in educational settings. *Educational Psychology Review, 7*(1), 1–6.

Guerra, N. G., Tolan, P. H., & Hammond, W. R. (1996). Prevention and treatment of adolescent violence. In L. D. Eron, J. H. Gentry, & P. Schlegel (Eds.), *Reason to HOPE: A psychosocial perspective on violence and youth* (pp. 383–403). Washington, DC: American Psychological Association.

Hakim, L. (1992). *Conflict resolution in schools.* San Rafael, CA: Human Rights Resource Center.

Hamner, C. J. (1993, Winter). Youth violence: Gangs on Main Street. *Issues in Brief,* pp. 1–8.

Hawkins, D. F. (1996). *Ethnicity, race, class and adolescent violence* (Center Paper 006). Boulder, CO: Center for the Study and Prevention of Violence.

Heymann, P. (1996). *Saving our children: Can youth violence be prevented?* (Published proceedings of the Harvard Law School Center for Criminal Justice Interdisciplinary Conference). Cambridge, MA: Harvard Law School.

Hoffman, A. M., & Summers, R. W. (1996). The anatomy of gangs. In A. M. Hoffman (Ed.), *Schools, violence and society* (pp. 33–43). Westport, CO: Praeger.

Huff, C. R., & Trump, K. S. (1996). Youth violence and gangs. *Education and Urban Society, 26*(4), 492–502.

Jacobson, M., & Lombard, R. (1992). Effective school climate: Roles for peers, practitioners, and principals. *Rural Research Report, 3,* 1–6.

Johnson, D. W., & Johnson, R. T. (1995). *Reducing school violence through conflict resolution.* Alexandria, VA: Association for Supervision and Curriculum Development.

Katz, M. S., Noddings, N., & Strike, K. A. (1999). *Justice and caring.* New York: Teachers College Press.

Kirby, M. (1995). *Street smarts: Activities that help teenagers take care of themselves.* San Jose, CA: Resource Publications, Inc.

Lantieri, L., DeJong, W., & Dutrey, J. (1996). Waging peace in our schools. In A. M. Hoffman (Ed.), *Schools, violence, and society* (pp. 241–252). Westport, CT: Praeger.

Maxwell, J. (1989). Mediation in the schools: Self-regulation, self-esteem and self-discipline. *Mediation Quarterly, 7,* 149–155.

Monsey, B., Owen, G., Qierman, C., Lambert, L., & Hyman, V. (1995). *What works in preventing rural violence.* St. Paul, MN: Amherst H. Wilder Foundation.

Petersen, G. J., Beckley, C. Z., Speaker, K. M., & Pietrzak, D. (1998). An examination of violence in three rural school districts. *The Rural Educator, 19*(3), 25–32.

Phillips, N. K. (1997). *Children in the urban environment.* Springfield, IL: Thomas.

Poland, S. (1999, October). *School crisis and youth violence.* Paper presented at the Meadows Principal Improvement and Professional Development Program, Commerce, TX.

Posner, M. (1994). Research raises troubling questions about violence prevention programs. *Harvard Education Letter, 10*(3), 1–4.

Prothrow-Stith, D. B. (1995). The epidemic of youth violence in America: Using public health prevention strategies to prevent violence. *Journal of Health Care for the Poor and Underserved, 6*(6), 95–101.

Sapphire, P. (1999). Know ALL your students to reduce violence. *The Education Digest, 65*(1), 4–5.

Schomberg, R. (1992). *A developmental approach to conflict resolution.* Paper based on presentation at the Annual Conference of the National Association for the Education of Young Children, Anaheim, CA.

Schroth, G., & Dunbar, R. (1993). Mission possible: One school's journey to site-based education. *Catalyst for Change, 23,* 24–26.

Sergiovanni, T. J. (1995). *The principalship.* Boston: Allyn & Bacon.

Sommers, I., & Baskin, D. R. (1994). Factors related to female adolescent initiation into violent street crime. *Youth and Society, 25*(4), 468–489.

Stephens, R. D. (1995). *Safe schools: A handbook for violence prevention.* Bloomington, IN: National Education Service.

Tolan, P. H., Guerra, N. G., & Kendall, P. C. (1995). A developmental-ecological perspective on antisocial behavior in children and adolescents: Toward a unified risk and intervention framework. *Journal of Consulting and Clinical Psychology, 63*(4), 579–584.

Trotter, J. C. (1993). *Teen stress: How to cope.* Atlanta, GA: Wholistic Stress Control Institute.

Vocational Foundation, Inc. (1978). *Our turn to listen: A White Paper on unemployment, education and crime based on extensive interviews with New York City teenage dropouts.* New York: Author. (ERIC Document Reproduction Service No. ED152871).

Walker, H. M., & Gresham, F. M. (1997). Making schools safer and violence free. *Intervention in School and Clinic, 32*(4), 199–204.

Walker, H. M., Irvin, L. K., & Sprague, J. R. (1997). Violence prevention and school safety: Issues, problems, approaches, and recommended solutions. *OSSC Bulletin, 41*(1), 6–20.

Wright, J. D., Sheley, J. F., & Smith, M. D. (1992). Kids, guns, and killing fields. *Transaction Social Science and Modern Society, 30*(1), 84–89.

Wubbles, W. (1992). Do teacher ideals distort the self reports of their interpersonal behavior? *Teaching and Teacher Education, 8*(1), 47–58.

Zigler, E., Taussig, C., & Black, K. (1992). Early childhood intervention: A promising preventative for juvenile delinquency. *American Psychologist, 47,* 997–1006.

4

Violence and School Principals

Edward H. Seifert
Texas A&M University-Commerce

Buzz, a student in a small community of 4,500 people, walked into his first-period class at Walker Middle School with a loaded .38-caliber handgun hidden in his backpack. Shortly after the class began Buzz removed the handgun from his backpack, stood up, and pointed the gun at the teacher and 26 students. He yelled, "I am holding you hostage." A teacher walking down the hall saw what was happening and immediately contacted Ms. Mary Boswell, the principal. Boswell had the secretary notify the police and activated the campus crisis management plan. The code for a building lockdown was heard over the school intercom and Boswell headed for the hostage classroom. When she arrived at the classroom door she could see fear on the faces of everyone in the classroom. Boswell began talking to the student holding the gun and called him by name. She knew Buzz—he was an academically talented student and a member of the Walker Middle School academic decathlon team. After some negotiations, Buzz agreed to free the student and teacher hostages in exchange for Principal Boswell. Buzz, with his hostage, moved from the classroom to Boswell's office and continued to point his gun at the principal. As Principal Boswell talked with Buzz, he began to tell her his problems. Boswell listened and continued to suggest that Buzz hand her the gun. After 6 hours Buzz gave the gun to Principal Boswell and the hostage crisis was over with no physical harm.

At one point during this situation 12 satellite dishes were located on the streets surrounding Walker Middle School. Every major news organization in the country was on-site providing up-to-the-minute information with live on-air reports that included news about students still in the building.

Panic-stricken parents did not know whether or not their children were hostages. Fear was rampant.

The proliferation of 24-hour news channels with airtime to fill has changed the way news is delivered to the public. Most of the school violence situations reported on these newscasts focus on the perpetrators and not the victims. So, within minutes, television pictures of the Walker Middle School situation were live on millions of television screens around the world.

Research on school violence focuses primarily on the causes of student-initiated violence and strategies for prevention. Data are gathered concerning student and parent violence directed at teachers with less attention given to discovering the types of violence school principals face as they go about their daily work. In this chapter the types and incidents of violence perpetrated on campus principals are discussed along with some strategies for de-escalating violent situations.

THE EXTENT OF THE VIOLENCE

The Milton S. Eisenhower Foundation released the results of a research study that found violence in the late 1990s to be more prevalent than it was in 1969 (Lichtblau, 1999). Additionally, a person living in the United States is more likely to die from a violent crime than in any other industrialized country in the world. Although the Eisenhower report contains disturbing news, some might dismiss the report as research gone wrong. Appropriate questions arise, "How much violence is there in society and how does that violence affect the workplace and schools in particular?"

For the past 15 years workplace violence has surfaced as a real concern for the business community and it continues to be a growing problem for employees and employers. According to a 1993 Northwestern National Life study, 25% of workers have been assaulted, threatened, or harassed while at work. In the same study, more than 2 million workers reported being attacked, 6.3 million were threatened, and 16.1 million workers were harassed. If this study is representative of society as a whole, the fact that schools are facing the same types of behavior is not surprising.

Schools reflect their surroundings. The types and amount of violence students bring to the campus is a direct reflection of what they experience at home, on the street, in their religious communities, and with their peers. Educators must be able to cope with ramifications of fear generated by incidents in schools from Alaska to Georgia. Karen Kleinz (1998) stated that the fear of school violence is legitimate, but the focus of this fear should be placed on society and the frenzy surrounding these incidents created by the electronic and print media. Violence perpetrated by children upon children sends up a flare, warning of a systemic change in society that schools alone cannot heal. To indicate otherwise is misguided and detrimental to solving the violence problems schools face daily.

At present violence in schools is a major concern for students, parents, teachers, and administrators. In a 1993 survey, 93% of the adults indicated that violence against students and teachers in elementary and secondary schools was a concern and 70% of these respondents indicated that they were "very concerned" (Thompson, 1994). The magnitude of the concern is demonstrated by the results showing that school violence is a bigger concern (91%) than concerns over academic standards (Thompson, 1994). Today's parents are concerned that their children are no longer safe at school and fear their child might become the next victim.

The Safe Schools Survey (1998) revealed that students frequently experience school violence. Sixty percent of the respondents reported observing violence anywhere from one to five times during the school year, 66% revealed being verbally insulted, 39% had property stolen from them, and 19% were kicked, bitten, or hit. One of the most disturbing aspects of this Safe Schools Survey is that 59% of respondents reported being victims of violent acts, although they failed to report the incidents to a principal, teacher, or any other adult associated with the school.

National statistics provide a broader view. In a report titled *Violence and School Discipline Problems in U.S. Public Schools* (1998), Volokh and Snell stated that approximately 1,000 crimes per 100,000 students occurred in public schools between 1996 and 1997. As one would expect, crime was more prevalent in high schools—103 crimes per 100,000 students. Elementary schools on the other hand had only 13 crimes per 100,000 students. How violence is defined in these studies affects numbers and percentages; however, it appears violence and crime on school campuses is an issue to be addressed (Volokh & Snell, 1998).

VIOLENCE DIRECTED TOWARD TEACHERS

Research on school violence and prevention focuses primarily on student safety and identification of students with behaviors that may be manifested in violence toward other students. As schools struggle to limit the effects of school violence on students, other actors on the school stage merit attention. Teachers appear to be the victims of student rage, insubordination, rape, and assault. In 1993 the Saskatchewan Teachers Association surveyed their membership, finding that more than 40% of the respondents stated that they had suffered one or more instances of abuse (Thompson, 1994). The abuse types were primarily verbal, rude gestures, and slanderous statements, but 12% of the respondents reported damage to personal property and 9% reported more than one incident of damage. Thompson found that 98% of the teachers responding to a school violence survey had experienced physical abuse. Two percent had been physically abused by their own family members and 7% had experienced threats of violence. Twenty-nine percent of the violent actions against teachers were perpetrated by students against their own classroom teacher, 18% were by students who were not in the victim's (a teacher) class, and 15% were initiated by a student's parents. Thirty-eight percent reported no student violence. These data indicate that teachers are not immune to violence at schools.

Race and gender of teachers experiencing violence was documented by *The Metropolitan Life Survey of the American Teacher, 1999: Violence in America's Schools—Five Years Later* (Binns, 1999). The 1999 study showed that 45% of teacher victims were male and 55% were female. Eighty-five percent of the teachers were Anglo, 5% African American, and 4% Hispanic. About 27% of the elementary teachers were victims of violence, whereas 60% of the secondary teachers faced violent acts by students and parents.

Teachers' concerns are changing. Volokh and Snell (1998) compared the top seven disciplinary problems facing teachers in 1940 with those problems facing teachers in 1990. In 1940 the major problems were talking out of turn, chewing gum, making noise, running in the hall, cutting in line, dress code violations and littering, as compared with the 1990 problems of drug abuse, alcohol abuse, pregnancy, suicide, rape, robbery, and assault. The Metropolitan Life survey (Binns, 1999) supports the trend outlined by Volokh and Snell revealing that one in six teachers (17%) in 1999 were the victim of violent acts at school as compared to one in nine teachers (11%) in 1993.

VIOLENCE DIRECTED TOWARD PRINCIPALS

Violence perpetrated against principals receives little attention. Principals themselves may contribute to this lack of interest by underreporting the violence directed toward them at school. In order to establish a clearer understanding of violence directed toward administrators, 210 randomly selected building principals in Texas completed a 64-item survey.

The survey items were categorized as being: (a) threats from parents or guardians, or (b) threats from students. Within the first category the items were further classified as interactions with parents or guardians, nonverbal intimidation by parents or guardians, and physical contact with parents or guardians. Threats from students were similarly classified. Principals were asked to check items on the survey that they had experienced in the past year.

Eighty-eight percent of the principals indicated that the statement, "I am calling the superintendent" was made to them. Another 80.5% indicated they had been threatened with, "I will be calling my attorney." Thirty-two percent of the respondents were told, "This will cost you your job." These results suggest that parents or guardians indeed verbally threaten principals. Do principals not view such parent behavior as threatening or having potential for violence, or is it possible that principals have come to accept such behavior as simply part of the job?

Principals' reports of parents or guardians use of vulgarity and nonverbal intimidation were examined as well. Fifty-three percent of the principals indicated that parents or guardians had directed vulgar language and disrespect toward them in a very personal manner. Thirty-nine percent of the respondents said that parents or guardians had slammed the office door and/or banged objects on the principal's desk and more than 17% of the principals reported parents invading their personal space by physically moving in close to them. Such parent or guardian behaviors should cause principals to fear for their personal safety and question the impact of such conduct on the school as a whole.

The respondents reported few incidents of parents or guardians physically attacking principals. In this Texas study, hitting, shoving, or physically grabbing the principal was reported by 6 of the 210 principals who responded to the survey. Although the number is small, any physical violence between parents and school principals is inappropriate.

Students as well as parents threaten principals. Thirty percent of the principals in this study reported that a student stated to them, "I will be calling my attorney," and 28% had been told by a student, "I am calling the superintendent." More than 20% of the respondents reported students had damaged or destroyed their private property (home, auto, etc.).

Vulgarity and nonverbal intimidation seem to be the threat of choice for students. Fifty-six percent of the principals reported students had directed vulgar language and behaved disrespectfully toward them. Another 43% said that students had slammed the principal's office door and/or slammed or banged objects on the principal's desk. Over 15% of the respondents indicated that students had invaded their personal space.

Threatening physical contact between students and principals is unacceptable in all situations. Self-defense by principals may be appropriate, but aggressive action on the part of a school administrator will always be viewed negatively. In this study, 6% of the principals indicated that a student had physically shoved them and 5% reported being hit by a student. Again, the numbers are not large, but threatening student behavior toward a school principal should raise concerns for educators and society as a whole.

The results of this principal survey indicate that threatening behavior toward principals from both students and parents does occur. Today these behaviors might be accepted as ordinary, but unfortunate, aspects of the principal's job. Yet giving parents and students the psychological energy to threaten through intimidation opens the door to physical violence and should not be tolerated by any individual, particularly principals. Inappropriate behavior toward the principal undermines the principal's authority and directly impacts the climate and culture of the school organization.

STRATEGIES FOR DE-ESCALATION
OF VIOLENT SITUATIONS

A campus principal cannot predict when and where violence may strike, but administrators must be prepared. A proactive stance includes mastering conflict management skills and understanding the causes for anger.

A positive school atmosphere is important for avoiding and resolving conflict. Principals can help establish a healthy school climate by dealing with all problems honestly and openly. Additionally, beginning each contact with teachers, parents, and students in a positive manner, even when the issues at hand are emotional, is one method of modeling acceptable behavior.

The principal can also establish a healthy tone by developing strong communication skills. In his book, *The Eight Essential Steps to Conflict Resolution* (1992), Dudley Weeks outlined some "doables"—those actions that have a good chance of being successful. One of the "doables" that Weeks suggested principals integrate into their "tool kit" for avoiding violent situations is a willingness to be an empathetic listener. This does not mean agreement but does mean understanding. Additionally, when communicating with potentially violent people, generating options and looking for common ground can defuse a volatile situation. Using combative language or gestures is not conducive to healthy communication.

Principals can circumvent violent situations by avoiding adversarial entanglements. First the elements upon which everyone agrees should be identified and then energy directed at solving the disputed issues. Weeks (1999) suggested developing an "our" rather than an "I" attitude. The "I" approach can result in a power struggle between the principal and parents and students with resulting mistrust and conflict. Principals are granted authority by the board of trustees but open displays of power in volatile situations is not judicious.

The Illinois State Police (2000) suggested some strategies for avoiding violence in the workplace. These strategies are particularly applicable to schools and principals:

- Do not try to diagnose the problem immediately.
- Don't moralize. Be factual and honest.
- Don't be confused by sympathetic gestures.
- Don't ignore the possibility that mishandled problems will become violent.
- Do make it clear you want to solve the problem.
- Do make sure that all parties in the potential violent situation know the facts of the situation.

CONCLUSION

School violence is often directed at teachers and students, but principals are victims as well, although such acts are less often the focus of research. Additional data are needed to determine the true extent of violence directed at school administrators. As the chief executive officer, the principal sets the tone for the entire school. When inappropriate and sometimes violent behavior occurs in the front office, why should students not expect to find the same behavior acceptable throughout the school?

CHAPTER ACTIVITIES

For Discussion

- Discuss the Walker Middle School situation, listing those strategies that Principal Boswell did well and those upon which she could improve?
- What evidence demonstrates that school violence is escalating and what is the situation on your campus?
- What strategies have been implemented on the campus where you work to prevent teacher-directed violence?
- What strategies can principals utilize to protect themselves from violence perpetrated by parents, guardians, and students? How can principals model the behavior they wish to see exhibited by teachers, students, and parents?
- How does societal violence impact school personnel? Describe the types of violence you have experienced in society and on the school campus.

Case Study

You are the principal of Cameron High School. Cameron is a medium-size suburban school in a socially conservative community. Today at 9:30 a.m. you will be meeting with Mr. Herman Kline, former mayor of the city of Cameron, to discuss your recommendation to expel his daughter, Hilda. On several occasions Hilda made veiled verbal threats toward teachers, other students, and, on two occasions, toward Ms. Jackson, the assistant principal at Cameron High. The incident that precipitated this meeting was Hilda's verbal and physical threat to harm Ms. Sharpton, her foreign-language teacher. As the principal, you are fully aware of Mr. Kline's reputation for being aggressive both verbally and physically, having dealt with him concerning his children in prior years.

Questions.

- What should you as the principal do to prepare for this meeting?
- What strategies would you employ to make sure the meeting does not escalate into a threatening and violent situation?
- How will the outcome of this meeting impact the teachers and students?
- Will the outcome affect the climate of the school?

REFERENCES

Binns, K. (1999). *The Metropolitan Life Survey of the American Teacher, 1999: Violence in America's public schools—years later* (Conducted by Louis Harris & Associates). New York: Metropolitan Life Insurance Company.

Illinois State Police. (2000). *Do's and don'ts for the supervision.* Retrieved January 2000, from http://www.isp.state.il.us/

Kleinz, K. (1998). *Never say never: Violence and tragedy can strike anywhere.* Retrieved December 2001 from http://www.naesp.org/misc/violence.htm

Lichtblau, E. (1999, December 6). Violence, poverty, worsening, report says. *Fort Worth Star-Telegram,* p. A5.

Northwestern National Life Study. (1993). *Combating work place violence.* Retrieved from January 2001 from http://www.isp.state.il.us/

Safe Schools Survey 1998. (1998). Retrieved December 2001, from www.ag.state.mn.us/home/classroom/safeschools1998/default.html

Thompson, L. (1994). *One incident is too many: Policy guidelines for safe schools.* Retrieved January 2001 from http://www.ssta.sasknet.com/research/school_improvement/94-05.htm

Volokh, A., & Snell, L. (1998*). School violence prevention: Strategies to keep schools safe.* Retrieved December 2001 from http://www.rppi.org/ps234.html

Weeks, D. (1999). *The eight essential steps to conflict resolution.* Los Angeles: Jeremy P. Tarcher.

II

SEEKING SOLUTIONS

5

Resolving Conflicts in Schools: An Educational Approach to Violence Prevention

Katharin A. Kelker
Montana State University–Billings

Butler Elementary School was built on school section land in 1906. The original white clapboard building is now surrounded by more modern brick structures that house kindergarten through fifth-grade classrooms. The playground looks out on wheat fields and clover meadows where Angus cattle graze. An idyllic scene. But what goes on inside is not always so ideal. Teachers complain that students are "disrespectful and prone to using foul language." Fistfights occur on the playground and some children feel intimidated by classmates who bully and harass them. Teachers say they no longer can count on parents supporting the school discipline system.

Is something unusual happening at Butler Elementary School? Are problems such as physical aggression, property damage, and incivility really on the rise in schools like Butler? Is school violence occurring in rural and suburban schools as well as in urban environments? According to the Clearinghouse on Urban Education (Schwartz, 1996), youth violence, which once was thought to be an urban public school problem and a consequence of poverty and family dysfunction, is actually experienced in stable suburban and rural communities and in some private schools as well. The Centers for Disease Control and the U.S. Department of Education, Department of Justice, and the National School Safety Center have examined homicides and suicides associated with schools, examining events occurring to and from school, as well as on both public or private school property, or while someone was on the way or going to an official school-sponsored event. The original study (Schwartz,1996) yielded these data:

- Less than 1% of all homicides among school-age children (5–19 years of age) occur in or around school grounds or on the way to and from school.
- 65% of school-associated violent deaths were students; 11% were teachers or other staff members; and 23% were community members who were killed on school property.
- 83% of school homicide or suicide victims were males.
- 28% of the fatal injuries happened inside the school building; 36% occurred outdoors on school property; and 35% occurred off campus.
- The deaths included in this study occurred in 25 states across the country and happened in both primary and secondary schools and in communities of all sizes.

Beginning with the killing at school of two girls in Pearl, Mississippi, in October 1997 and 2 months later a student opening fire on a prayer group in Paducah, Kentucky, several widely publicized school slayings occurred in small rural or suburban communities, including Edinboro, Pennsylvania; Springfield, Oregon; Fayetteville, Tennessee; and Littleton, Colorado. These frightening events triggered a strong reaction among policymakers and citizens throughout the country. School safety became a buzzword and violence prevention became a priority issue for local school boards (Hyman & Snook, 1999).

Because of these highly publicized shootings, the popular perception may be that schools are plagued and sometimes controlled by disruptive, disrespectful students who are too often violent. But the reality is something quite different. Student violence, whether in rural or urban environments, is vastly overreported and exaggerated. The National Center for the Study of Corporal Punishment and Alternatives (NCSCPA) at Temple University has been collecting data on school violence since the 1970s (Hyman & Snook, 1999). Their data show that school violence has not increased during the last 30 years. In fact, in recent years it has decreased, as has the overall crime rate. For instance, the FBI's annual statistical report on crime released in October 1999 indicates that juvenile arrests for serious crimes dropped nearly 11% between 1997 and 1998 (Lichtblau, 1999). The U.S. Department of Education (1999) reported that despite recent violent episodes in school settings, "most school crime is theft, not serious violent crime." Referring to school shootings, for which there are no reliable statistics prior to the mid-1990s, data show that such crimes have dropped from 55 in the 1992–1993 school year to around 40 in 1997–1998 (Hyman & Snook, 1999). Of course, this number is still unacceptable; even one death is too many, but given a national school population of over 50 million students, the current death rate does not represent an epidemic.

Though school violence cannot be documented as increasing dramatically in recent years, unfortunately what has increased is the use of guns, the tendency of younger children to commit more horrific crimes, and the national media coverage of local school murders, particularly in White suburban and rural communities (Hyman & Snook, 1999).

SCHOOL VIOLENCE VARIABLES

Rates of school violence seem to vary with school enrollment, with larger schools more likely to experience violent crime. For example during the 1996–1997 school year, one third of schools having more than 1,000 students experienced at least one serious violent crime compared to just 4% to 9% of schools with fewer than 1,000 students ("Safe Schools," 1998). So rural and suburban schools, because they tend to be smaller and not located in high-crime areas, have a better chance of creating positive learning environments.

But positive school climate is apparently not an automatic condition of location in a nonurban setting. As the teachers at Butler Elementary school in the opening vignette have noted, incivility, bullying, and harassment occur in small, rural schools and may contribute to an atmosphere of tension and unrest. Bryngelson and Cline (1998) suggested that instances of violence develop along a continuum that starts with simple discourtesy but, if not addressed, can escalate to bullying, harassment, physical abuse, hate crimes, and even murder (see Fig. 5.1).

RESPONSES TO SCHOOL VIOLENCE

Though rural and suburban schools inherently may be at less risk for violence, they are not immune to conflict. Like all schools and human institutions, nonurban schools experience conflict—student versus student, student versus teacher, teacher versus teacher, teacher versus parent. The concern is not to eliminate any sign of conflict but to create a school climate in which conflicts can be resolved in healthy ways. Especially in today's climate of concern over school violence, all schools must make safety a high priority and make a conscious effort to teach problem-solving and negotiation skills that build a framework for cooperation and the cultivation of mutual respect.

Social-Skills Instructional Models.   Widespread concern about youth violence has led to the development of numerous programs intended to prevent it. The U.S. Department of Education's (1998) document on safe schools suggests several types of prevention programs, including peer mediation, conflict resolution, problem solving, and anger management. Un-

Using force to injure, hurt, threaten, or take advantage of someone or do harm
  to property or the physical environment.
What kinds of violence occur most frequently in your school?
What kinds of violence worry you the most in your school?
What would you add, rearrange, or delete from this continuum?

Suicide
Murder
Rape
Terrorist Acts
Gangs
Hate Crimes
Weapons
Abusive Drinking and Drugs
Physical Abuse
Sexual Harassment
Stealing
Property Damage and Vandalism
Threats and Intimidation
Bullying
Trash Talk
Put Downs and Prejudice
Disrespect
Discourtesy
Begin—Ignoring

Note. From Bryngelson and Cline (1998). Copyright 1998 by Jim Bryngelson
and Sharon Cline, 1144 Henry Road, Billings, Montana 59102. Adapted by
permission.

FIG. 5.1.   A violence continuum.

fortunately, few of these programs have been thoroughly evaluated for
efficacy. Samples and Aber (1998) conducted an extensive review of the
data on school-based violence prevention programs, and they concluded
that many of these programs look promising but they have not been studied systematically enough to determine which methods are the most effective in reaching prevention goals. There is some evidence, however, that a
comprehensive, developmental approach of education and skill building
may be the most effective approach toward influencing attitudes and behavior (Lumsden, 2001).

    The basic premise of social-skills instruction models is that differences of
opinion and conflicts are bound to occur among adults and children in a
school environment. Because conflict is inevitable, educators and students
need to understand the dynamics of conflict and be prepared to manage
disagreements in constructive ways. Educators can prepare themselves by

developing and practicing conflict resolution skills like communication and collaborative problem solving. Students can receive training at their developmental level in social skills, problem solving, and peaceful conflict resolution. Table 5.1 presents three examples of conflict resolution activities designed to meet the developmental needs of primary, intermediate, and middle school students.

An example of a violence prevention, social-skills curriculum is the Second Step program, which is widely used with preschool through ninth-grade students. Research on the Second Step program has shown that implementation of this curriculum decreased the frequency of aggressive behaviors in third graders whereas these behaviors increased among control peer groups. The positive effects persisted for at least 6 months (M. Kaufman, Walker, & Sprague, 1997).

The Second Step program provides three levels of instruction from the most general to the most specific and supportive. The first level of intervention, which is designed for all students in the school community, focuses on teaching conflict resolution and anger management skills, as well as providing education about how to avoid drug and alcohol use.

Second-level intervention is designed for students identified as being at risk of engaging in antisocial behavior. This level emphasizes direct instruction in moral reasoning and impulse control.

The third and most intensive level of intervention is designed to meet the needs of students who already exhibit antisocial behavior patterns. At this level, various types of services and support are "wrapped around" the student and the student's family depending on their specific needs. The family is a partner in the needs-assessment process, rather than merely a passive recipient of services professionals deem appropriate.

Law Enforcement Models. Responding to perceived increases in school violence, schools have increasingly adopted law enforcement rather than educational models for violence reduction. These measures include the use of metal detectors, increased police presence in schools, searches of lockers and students, student and staff I.D. cards, a ban on the use of beepers on school grounds, school uniforms, boot camps, mandatory sentencing, and adjudicating delinquent adolescents as if they were adults. Whether or not these measures are effective in preventing violence is yet to be demonstrated (Gellert, 1997). However, a national study that compared violent and safe schools demonstrated that safe schools were characterized, not by police presence or the use of police tactics, but by leadership that instilled in students "a sense of fairness, belonging, and empowerment to effect change" (Elias, Lantieri, Janet, Walberg, & Zins, 1999). In this study, it was not the strict, authoritarian, rule-bound schools that were the safest, but the schools where adults modeled and students practiced respect and tolerance.

TABLE 5.1
Examples of Three Levels of Social-Skills/Peacemaking Training Activities

Preschool
Hand Hugs
Sometimes children can benefit from having a physical connection with each other. An activity like the hand hug can be used to end an activity or before children leave to go home. These kinds of brief contact experiences can restore good feelings to a group and remind children that they are part of a community.

Have the children stand in a circle with you, holding hands. Squeeze the hand of the child on your right. Have that child squeeze the hand of the child on his or her right, and so on, passing the hand hug around the circle. The hand hug stops when it comes back to you.

K–6
Bridges
Procedure:

1. Have partners of approximately equal size stand facing each other about six inches apart. Hands should be raised to shoulder level, with palms facing the partner's palms.

2. The players simultaneously fall forward, catching and supporting each other with their hands. They are now forming a bridge.

3. Pushing off each other, the players return to their original positions. Each player than moves back two inches, and the game continues as above.

4. The object is always for the players to catch and support each other as they fall. They can move as far apart as feels comfortable for them.
Despite its rather hair-raising appearance, this game offers very little opportunity for anyone to get hurt. Keep a watchful eye on things, however.

Middle School
Mirroring
Have students work in pairs. One person is A, the other is B. Partners should stand, facing one another. First B reflects all movements initiated by A, head to foot, including facial expressions. After a short time, call "change," so that positions are reversed. Then B initiates the actions and A reflects. Have students discuss what it was like to mirror another person's actions.

Note. The preschool examples are from Kreidler and Whittall (1999). Reprinted with permission from "Early Childhood Adventures in Peacemaking," by William J. Kreidler 1999. Published by Educators for Social Responsibility. For more information, call 1-800-370-2515. The K–6 examples are from Kreidler (1984). Adapted by permission. The middle school examples are from Kreidler (1994). Reprinted with permission from "Conflict Resolution in the Middle School," by William J. Kreidler 1994. Published by Educators for Social Responsibility. For more information, call 1-800-370-2515.

School Climate Models. Research on school safety supports the premise that no one method of intervention or prevention is likely to be effective. Instead indicators have been identified (American Psychological Association, 1993) that explain why some schools tend to be safer than others, depending on the presence or absence of certain characteristics at the school level. Several elements of the school culture and climate act as either protective factors or risk factors, decreasing or heightening a school's tendency to be safe or unsafe.

School-based risk factors include the following:

- Poor physical design and use of school space.
- Overcrowding.
- Lack of caring but firm disciplinary procedures.
- Insensitivity and poor accommodation to multicultural factors.
- Student alienation.
- Rejection of at-risk or "different" students by teachers and peers.
- Anger and resentment at school routines and demands for conformity.

Conversely, characteristics of the school culture and climate that serve a protective function include the following:

- Positive school climate and atmosphere.
- Clear and high performance expectations for all students.
- Inclusionary values and practices throughout the school.
- Strong student bonding to the school environment and the educational process.
- Provision of opportunities for skill acquisition and social development.

Elias and colleagues (1999) pointed out that safe schools are places where the school culture is such that all students can learn and feel comfortable. In creating such a positive school climate, rural schools do have some advantages. Historically, urban schools have had a much higher rate than rural schools of physical violence. Students in urban schools, for example, are nine times more likely than their rural peers and twice as likely as students in suburban schools to die violently at school (P. Kaufman, Hamburg, & Williams, 1998). Reiss and Roth (1993) noted that violence rates in secondary schools are highest in areas with higher crime rates and more street gangs, likely reflecting the situation in the surrounding community.

TEACHER TRAINING IN PEACEMAKING

Creating a school climate in which conflicts can be settled in prosocial ways does seem to involve the infusion of social-skills training into the daily school experiences of students, starting at an early age. Teachers are, of course, integral to this education process. In a sense, as Kreidler (1984) said, a teacher is a "peacemaker." Conflicts occur in the classroom and students look to teachers for guidance and modeling in how conflicts should be resolved. Kreidler suggested there are six basic causes for conflict in the classroom:

- Competitive atmosphere.
- Intolerant atmosphere.
- Poor communication.
- Inappropriate expression of emotion.
- Lack of conflict resolution skills.
- Misuse of power.

When any one of these types of conflict arises, teachers are expected to respond to them and restore order. With or without encouragement, students often bring their conflicts to the teacher for resolution. Left on their own, they sometimes get trapped in power struggles with peers. Appealing to adult authority is easier and often more immediately effective than trying to solve problems by themselves.

Even though teachers receive training in different discipline techniques, rarely is there anything in their education that helps them to understand conflict or develop skills necessary for teaching children how to make peace. Teachers cannot teach what they do not know and practice themselves. Communication, "emotional banking," and collaborative problem solving are all skills that teachers can learn, practice, and model for their students.

As part of the whole process of creating a safe school environment and inculcating mutual respect, teachers themselves need skills in keeping conflict within bounds. Even though disagreements and differences of opinion are inevitable, conflict does not have to be destructive or hurtful. Mastery of two interpersonal skills—communication and emotional "banking"—can help to keep conflicts within bounds and keep dialogue focused on problem solving rather than blaming.

Communication

In a conflict situation, people need to keep talking so barriers to communication should be avoided if at all possible. Communication barriers are high-risk responses, that is, responses whose impact on communication is frequently, though not inevitably, negative. These roadblocks—in and of themselves—are more likely to be destructive when one or more persons are interacting under stress. According to Bolton (1979), "Communication blocks are many and varied. They frequently diminish the other's self esteem. They tend to trigger defensiveness, resistance, and resentment. They can lead to dependency, withdrawal, feelings of defeat or of inadequacy" (p. 15).

What specific barriers are apt to hinder a dialogue? Pioneers in interpersonal communication like Carl Rogers (1970), Haim Ginott (1965), and Jack Gibb (1961) have pinpointed three types of responses that tend to block conversation—judging, sending solutions, and avoiding the other's concerns. Thomas Gordon (1970) summarized these findings in a comprehensive list that he called the "dirty dozen" of communication spoilers. These undesirable responses:

- Criticizing—Making a negative evaluation of other persons, their actions, or attitudes.
- Name Calling—Putting down or stereotyping the other person.
- Diagnosing—Analyzing why persons are behaving as they do; playing amateur psychologist.
- Praising Evaluatively—Making a global positive judgment of other persons, their actions, or attitudes as in "You are always such good girls."
- Ordering—Commanding the other person to do what you want to have done.
- Threatening—Trying to control the other's action by warning of negative consequences that you will instigate.
- Moralizing—Telling another person what he or she should do; preaching.
- Excessive or Inappropriate Questioning—Closed-ended questions requiring few words to answer (e.g., Are you sorry for what you did?).
- Advising—Giving other persons "canned" solutions to their problems.
- Diverting—Pushing the other person's problems aside through distraction.
- Logical Argument—Attempting to convince other people with an appeal to facts or logic, usually without consideration of the emotional factors involved.
- Reassuring—Trying to stop the other persons from feeling the negative emotions they are experiencing.

Example.   Here is an example of how a teacher managed conflict with a parent by avoiding communication barriers and using reflective listening and communication skills. As a first-year special-education teacher, Mary tried to be positive with all of the parents of her students. But one father, Mr. Vossler, never seemed to be satisfied and Mary became resentful of his attitude. "Doesn't he know how much effort I put into helping his son, Josh" Mary wondered.

Because Mary resented this father, she started avoiding him. One night, however, Mary found herself in the grocery checkout line right behind Mr. Vossler. As soon as he spotted Mary, Mr. Vossler began to berate her in a complaining voice. Mary wanted to leave her groceries and run out of the store, but something made her stay and listen without getting defensive. What was he saying? What did he really want?

Mary controlled her tendency to jump into the conversation and cut off Mr. Vossler's tirade. Gradually she was able to reflect back to him the things he was saying. She became aware that Mr. Vossler was passionate about his son doing well in school and frustrated that Josh received low grades despite the help he received in special education.

Mary acknowledged Mr. Vossler's feelings of frustration and concern; she complimented him for caring so much about his son's education. They sat together on a bench in front of the grocery store and talked about strategies to help Josh achieve greater success in school.

Emotional Bank Account

In relationships with parents, students, and colleagues, teachers like Mary need to develop trust relationships based on many acts of kindness and repeated instances of listening and following through. When a trust relationship exists, then in times of conflict the parties can acknowledge differences of opinion without destroying the basic relationships.

A metaphor that describes this process of building trust is the Emotional Bank Account (Covey, 1989). We all know what a financial bank account is. We make deposits into it and build up a reserve from which we can make withdrawals when we need to do so. An Emotional Bank Account operates similarly. A teacher can make deposits into an Emotional Bank Account through courtesy, kindness, honesty, and keeping commitments. Consistently behaving toward another person in a courteous, honest, and reliable way builds up a reserve of trust. If the trust level is high enough, then the teacher can call upon that trust when conflict situations occur. Colleagues, students, and parents will forgive mistakes or trust the teacher enough to try something new if there is already a history with that teacher of positive interactions. In other words, building a trust relationship and making "deposits" into an Emotional Bank Account creates an emotional reserve to compensate for "withdrawals" that may need to be made in times of conflict.

If a teacher has no prior relationship with a student, parent, or fellow teacher, then when conflict arises there may be no reserve of trust and the conflict may escalate. Or if the teacher has a habit of showing discourtesy or disrespect toward others, the teacher's Emotional Bank Account will quickly become "overdrawn" when there are disagreements with others.

Case Example. After Mary in the previous example had established a relationship with Mr. Vossler and made many deposits in his emotional bank account, she felt more confident when she needed to tell Mr. Vossler about something that was not going well for Josh. For example, one day Mary called Mr. Vossler to explain why she was keeping Josh after school. Josh was staying to redo a paper because Mary had caught him copying another student's work. Mary realized that Josh was unable to complete the assignment by himself because he did not understand what to do. She took time with Josh after school to assist him in understanding the directions and doing his best. Rather than becoming angry or upset, Mr. Vossler was supportive of Mary's management of Josh's problem and thanked her for informing him. With a history of mutual problem solving, Mary had won Mr. Vossler's trust and could deliver "bad news" without worrying about jeopardizing their relationship.

Collaborative Problem Solving

Probably the most sophisticated conflict resolution skill that a teacher can have is the ability to do collaborative problem solving. Collaborative problem solving is a specific group process for dealing with substantive issues in a conflict or disagreement. Participants in a collaborative problem-solving session must be committed to following the ground rules for discussion and to keeping focused on substantive solutions, rather a rehash of grievances.

Collaborative problem solving is not conceptualized in terms of a win/ lose strategy, and it does not produce an imposed solution. Instead collaborative problem solving involves all the members of the group in devising options, selecting the most promising option, and committing to trying the selected option. Thus, all participants are heard, all are decision makers, and all must buy into the final product of the group discussion, at least for an agreed-upon trial period.

Steps in Collaborative Problem Solving—Define Problem. Often the hardest part of problem solving is defining the problem in a way that is understood and accepted by all the members of the group. An inaccurate statement of the problem may undermine the entire collaborative problem-solving process so it is important to arrive at a clear, concrete, succinct statement (Bolton, 1979).

For an optimal outcome, the problem should be stated in terms of needs instead of solutions (Fisher & Ury, 1991). For example, a teacher may want to try a new method of reading, but this new method is not part of the school district's adopted curriculum. Her principal says she is not free to try "just any method," no matter how promising it may sound. So a conflict arises between what the teacher wants to do and what the principal thinks should happen. At this point, the principal could impose a solution to the conflict and "order" the teacher to comply with the school district's curriculum. However, imposing such a solution might well leave the teacher angry and dissatisfied with what she has to teach. In collaborative problem solving, the type of conflict would be resolved by focusing on the teacher's need to try something new and the principal's need to support the existing curriculum. Instead of sticking with the obvious solutions, collaborative problem solving would encourage the generation of a whole list of possibilities for meeting the needs of both parties.

Brainstorm Potential Solutions.   Brainstorming is defined as the rapid generation and listing of ideas or solutions without clarification and without evaluation of their merits. The process of brainstorming is used frequently in a variety of contexts. Unfortunately, because of this widespread use, brainstorming techniques are not always applied precisely and some of the key aspects of brainstorming are ignored (Frey & Barge, 1997).

In a collaborative problem-solving process, it is important to adhere to all of the basic principles of the brainstorming technique. These guidelines are designed to create a climate in which energies are focused on conceiving possible solutions in a short time period. Deviation from any of the guidelines may slow the flow of ideas and decrease the group's creativity. The essential rules for brainstorming are the following:

- Don't evaluate. Evaluation can thwart creativity because participants think they have to defend their ideas.
- Don't clarify. Explanatory remarks interfere with the rapid and creative generation of possible solutions.
- Go for "far out" ideas. A far-out idea may seem silly, but it may contain within it the seed of a potential solution. Also, zany ideas tend to break the tension and loosen up the group. People are freer to present any solution when they see that strange or unusual ideas are being included.
- List every idea. Don't leave anyone's idea out—even if it sounds bizarre. Unworkable solutions will quickly disappear as the winnowing process occurs.
- Avoid attaching people's names to ideas. Each person in the group puts forth ideas which trigger the thinking of others. In the end, no one has sole ownership of the collective wisdom of the group (Bolton, 1979).

Select Solutions and Check Consequences.   It is important not to come into a problem-solving session with the attitude that there is only one adequate solution to a conflict. There may be many solutions that will result in satisfactory outcomes. After the brainstorming session, the next step is clarification. Have the group review the list of ideas and identify any ideas that require clarification or rewording. The clarification should be as succinct as possible. The "no evaluation" guideline applies to the clarification period as well as to the generation of ideas (Bolton, 1979).

Once clarifications are complete, the selection process begins. This is not an effort to determine the one and only solution to the problem. Instead the group will be looking for all of the solutions that have potential.

Give the group an opportunity to review the list again. Identify any ideas that appear to be incomplete or redundant. See if there are some solutions that could be elaborated upon or combined.

The process of elaboration and combination will usually reduce the number of ideas on the list. Now the group can evaluate what proposed solution or combination of solutions will be selected for trial. Do not eliminate solutions one-by-one by going down the whole list. Instead use a process in which each member of the group has the opportunity to vote for one to three solutions that appear to be the most promising. Usually this voting process will eliminate some solutions and narrow the number of solutions still to be considered.

Once the choices have been narrowed to the ones most favored by members of the group, jointly decide on one or more of the alternatives to try. This decision should be made by consensus rather than by a majority vote. Consensus means finding a sense of the group—how willing the members of the group are to accept the group's decision, even though the particular solution is not an individual member's first choice. In a consensus-building process, there will be those who favor the solution and those who may be lukewarm about the solution but are still willing to "live with it" or give it a try.

Once the group has selected a solution that seems mutually desirable, it is then necessary to consider the possible consequences of that solution. Sometimes seemingly desirable solutions prove to be unworkable because of initially unforeseen consequences. Though it is impossible to predict all outcomes, the group should make the effort to surface any consequences that may make the chosen solution difficult or inappropriate to implement.

Make a Plan. Once a solution has been selected, the group can then turn its attention to making a specific plan for trying the solution. At this point the group must work out the nitty-gritty details of how the solution will be implemented. The members involved need to decide who will do what, where, and by when. It is helpful, too, to specify times when the people involved will get together to check how the implementation of the solution is going. In most situations, the plan that evolves should be written down so that the written version is available as a reminder of the agreements made.

Implement. Once the plan is ready, then it is time to take action and implement the chosen solution.

Evaluate. At the agreed-upon time, the group reconvenes to review how the plan has gone and to determine if the solution chosen has proved to be effective. If the evaluation is not a positive one, the group can then return to the list of proposed solutions, review them, and determine if another solution should be tried. (See Fig. 5.2 for a summary of the steps in collaborative problem solving.)

Collaborative problem solving responds to the fact that human beings are creatures of strong emotions who often have radically different perceptions and may have difficulty communicating clearly. Emotions typically become entangled with the objective facts of the situation. Taking positions

- Define problem
- Brainstorm solutions
- Select a promising solution
- Check out consequences of choice
- Design an implementation
- Implement the plan
- Evaluate results

FIG. 5.2.   Summary of steps in collaborative problem solving.

just makes this worse because people's egos become identified with their positions. Collaborative problem solving focuses, not on individual positions or points of view, but on multiple solutions to the problem. The participants see themselves as working side by side, attacking the problem, not each other.

Teachers who are trained in problem-solving skills can work with students to establish a sense of classroom community that will not only reduce conflict but also help children and youth respond constructively to conflict. Classroom-by-classroom efforts at developing violence prevention skills can address the Violence Continuum at the lowest level of incivility—discourtesy, harassment and bullying— and in this way prevent escalation into more risky and violent behavior. In the end a multifaceted program of climate building, student education, teacher preparation and support, administrative leadership, and parent and community involvement is necessary to ensure school safety in every school, including those in rural and suburban settings.

COMPREHENSIVE SCHOOL SAFETY PLAN

Going back to the opening vignette about Butler Elementary School, let's examine what a comprehensive climate-building and skills-training program might entail. Teachers have already identified some problem areas in school climate: disrespect toward adults and use of profane language. Also reported are fights on the playground and instances of bullying and harassment. Even more concerning, teachers and parents do not seem to be in agreement on what the discipline practices should be. Clearly the atmosphere at Butler Elementary is not what teachers and parents would like to have.

Needs Assessment.   Creating a safe and welcoming environment at Butler and correcting those problems that seem to be the most alarming will take time and effort on the part of staff, parents, community members, and students. No quick fix will make things right for all concerned. As a first step, Butler might undertake a School Climate Needs Assessment, asking questions of the stakeholders about how appropriate they perceive the atmosphere, level of civility, rules, and discipline at Butler to be. In addition to the needs assessment, an outside evaluation team of knowledgeable educators and community members could compile an assessment of the existing data on discipline and make note of any problem areas, including unsafe parts of the school building and grounds, unsupervised parts of the school day, and times when more significant behavior problems occur.

Building Safety Plan. Based on the data from the Needs Assessment and School Climate Profile, a task force of teachers, administrators, parents, and students can develop a School Climate-Building Plan, which addresses any necessary changes in school routines, supervision, management, or training for teachers and staff. This plan should be reviewed by the community and adopted officially by the Board of Education with action steps and timelines for implementation.

Behavioral Expectations. After a school safety plan has been developed and implemented, the next step in the climate-building process is a schoolwide discussion of behavioral expectations. Too often school discipline programs provide information about what the students are not supposed to do, but offer little information about what the students should do (Sprague, Sugai, & Walker, 1998). Identifying and communicating behavioral expectations gives students a clear idea of how they are supposed to act in a variety of school situations. The behavioral expectations should include simple good manners and a clear emphasis on students helping each other and demonstrating concern for the welfare of others.

The actual list of behavioral expectations at Butler will be uniquely designed by its constituents, but will probably contain elements that would be recognized as important parts of a safe school environment in any public school.

Once decided upon, behavioral expectations should be illustrated and widely posted in the school. How to behave appropriately should be modeled and demonstrated in every classroom and every activity throughout the school day. In other words, lunchroom behavior, how to wait in line, what to do on the playground, how to treat grown-ups, and the like, should be discussed, demonstrated, and reinforced multiple times every day. Parents and community members should also know about the school's behavioral expectations so that students are reinforced at home and elsewhere for their good manners and proper treatment of others.

Social Skills Curriculum. To help with the schoolwide effort at implementing behavioral expectations, Butler Elementary staff may want to consider adopting one of the curricula available for teaching problem solving and conflict resolution. If a commercial curriculum does not meet local needs, the faculty could develop its own curriculum and draw from a number of sources. In any case, whatever curriculum is chosen should be "spiral" in nature; that is, the same themes should be repeated several times in the K–12 grade levels with increasing sophistication at each subsequent level. The importance of having a consistent curriculum throughout the grade levels is to create a school environment where staff, students, and parents are familiar with the same problem-solving and conflict resolution vocabulary and techniques. As students move from grade to grade, they will learn more about problem solving, but the basic vocabulary will remain familiar and consistent. With a common language for problem solving and shared behavioral expectations, it should be easier to open up dialogue when conflicts arise.

Levels of Prevention. Setting behavioral expectations and teaching conflict resolution, emotional literacy, and anger management procedures constitutes what M. Kaufman et al.(1997) called the "umbrella of primary prevention." Such measures are intended expose all students, including typical students who do not have behavioral problems, to the basics of getting along with others. If Butler takes these basic steps, the school will probably see some positive changes in the general climate of the school. But primary prevention is probably not enough. Secondary prevention, designed for students who need more support than is offered on a schoolwide basis, must go further than group education. Secondary prevention involves individually tailored behavioral and academic supports for those students who have a history of not meeting behavioral expectations. Rather than just subjecting these students to disciplinary procedures and punishments, secondary prevention requires direct teaching of skills like moral reasoning and impulse control. Again, parents can be involved in these individual processes, so these at-risk students get the same kind of behavioral instruction at home as at school.

A third intensive level also must be available for any students that Butler identifies as having already exhibited a troubling pattern of antisocial behavior. Parents of these students will have to be included in planning individual interventions that may involve supportive mental health services, behavior management, and other services that can be implemented both at school and in the home. In rare cases, certain students may have to be placed in alternative settings where their individual emotional and behavioral needs can be met in a highly structured environment such as a specialized school or residential treatment center.

CONCLUSION

Butler Elementary can become the safe environment that staff, students, and parents want to have if everyone accepts some responsibility and commits to implementing a well-coordinated, comprehensive plan for prevention and intervention. School communities, whether in rural, suburban, or urban environments, are a reflection of their surroundings. If school safety is a high priority, then the community has to take ownership of the challenges involved in changing school climate and providing support to children with behavioral problems and the staff who work with them. A comprehensive school safety plan that includes teacher training and support, administrative adjustments, schoolwide behavioral expectations, multilevel prevention curriculum, and broad-based community involvement and support can make schools one of the safest and most rewarding places for children to be.

CHAPTER ACTIVITIES

For Further Discussion

1. When might you use the steps for collaborative problem solving? (Refer to Fig. 5.2—Summary of Steps in Collaborative Problem Solving.)
2. Are there circumstances when using this process might be inappropriate? (Provide specific examples along with a rationale for your response.)
3. When you use collaborative problem solving, what data might you collect to evaluate results? (Use your response to Question 1 as the circumstance for which you used the process and would collect data.)
4. How would you use the data to modify your original collaborative problem solutions? How might you use the data to modify the process itself?

Case Study

Reread the description of Butler Elementary School, which is the first paragraph of this chapter. You are the principal of Butler. A new superintendent has recently been hired for your district. One of her first mandates is that district schools must demonstrate parental involvement in developing a safe-school plan.

1. Identify the problem(s) in involving parents that you might face as principal of Butler Elementary. Who are the key stakeholders you would involve in planning for parent involvement in the safe-school effort?
2. How would you involve parents in every step of the Safe-School Plan, including assessing school climate and developing schoolwide behavioral expectation?
3. How would you include the media in the development of the Safe-School Plan? When would you begin to involve the media?

4. How do you see involving students the school climate assessment and in setting behavioral expectations?
5. Where would you go for ideas for behavioral expectations? How would you go about setting behavioral standards for each school environment and activity?
6. How long do you think it would take to complete a Safe-School Plan? Weeks? Months? Years? Explain your choice?
7. How would you go about evaluating the effectiveness of your Safe-School Plan once it has been implemented?
8. Would the development of a Safe-School Plan be different in an urban high school? A suburban middle school? How do location, level, or size of school influence the development of a Safe-School Plan?

REFERENCES

American Psychological Association, Commission on Youth Violence. (1993). *Violence and youth: Psychology's response.* Washington, DC: American Psychological Association.

Bolton, R. B. (1979). *People skills: How to assert yourself, listen to others, and resolve conflicts.* New York: Simon & Schuster.

Bryngelson, J., & Cline, S. (1998). *A violence continuum.* Billings, MT: CARE, Educators for Social Responsibility.

Covey, S. (1989). *The 7 habits of highly effective people: Restoring the character ethic.* New York: Fireside.

Elias, M., Lantieri, L., Janet, P., Walberg, H., & Zins, J. (1999, May 19). Violence is preventable. *Education Week,* pp. 45, 49.

Fisher, R., & Ury, W. (1991). *Getting to yes: Negotiating agreement without giving in* (2nd ed.). New York: Penguin Books.

Frey, L. R., & Barge, J. K. (Eds.). (1997). *Managing group life: Communicating in decision making groups.* New York: Houghton Mifflin.

Gellert, G. (1997). *Confronting violence.* Boulder, CO: Westview Press.

Gibb, J. (1961). Defense level and influence potential in small groups. In L. Petrullo & B. Bass (Eds.), *Leadership and interpersonal behavior* (pp. 66–81).New York: Holt, Rinehart & Winston.

Ginott, H. (1965). *Between parent and child: New solutions to old problems.* New York: Macmillan.

Gordon, T. (1970). *Parent effectiveness training: The "No-Lose" program for raising responsible children.* New York: Peter H. Wyden.

Hyman, I., & Snook, P. (1999). *Dangerous schools: What we can do about the physical and educational abuse of our children.* San Francisco: Jossey-Bass, Inc.

Kaufman, M., Walker, H., & Sprague, J. (1997). *Translating research on safe and violence free schools into effective practices.* Eugene, OR: Institute on Violence and Destructive Behavior.

Kaufman, P., Hamburg, B. A., & Williams, K. R. (Eds.), (1998). *Indicators of school crime and safety.* Washington, DC: U.S. Departments of Education and Justice.

Kreidler, W. (1984). *Creative conflict resolution: More than 200 activities for keeping peace in the classroom K–6.* Glenview, IL: Scott, Foresman.

Kreidler, W. (1994). *Conflict resolution in the middle school.* Cambridge, MA: Educators for Social Responsibility.

Kreidler, W., & Whittall, S. T. (1999). *Early childhood adventures in peacemaking.* Cambridge, MA: Educators for Social Responsibility.

Lichtblau, E. (1999, October 18). Juvenile crime rate continues to decrease. *Register Guard,* pp. 1A, 12A.

Lumsden, L. (Eds.), (2001). *Trends and issues: School safety and violence prevention.* Eugene: University of Oregon, ERIC Clearinghouse on Educational Management.

Reiss, A. J., & Roth, J. A. (1993). *Understanding and preventing violence.* Washington, DC: National Academy Press.

Rogers, C. (1970). *Carl Rogers on encounter groups.* New York: Harper & Row.

Safe schools, safe students: A guide to violence prevention strategies (1998). Washington, DC: Drug Strategies.

Samples, F., & Aber, L. (1998). Evaluations of school-based violence prevention programs. In D. S. Elliott, B. A. Hamburg, & K. R. Williams (Eds.), *Violence in American schools: A new perspective* (pp. 217–252). New York: Cambridge University Press.

Schwartz, W. (1996). *An overview of strategies to reduce school violence* (Digest No. 115). New York: Teachers College, ERIC Clearinghouse on Urban Education.

Sprague, J., Sugai, G., & Walker, H. (1998). Antisocial behavior in schools. In F. Gresham & T. S. Watson (Eds), *Handbook of child behavior therapy* (pp. 451–474). New York: Plenum.

Stephens, R. (1998). *Checklist of characteristics of youth who have caused school-associated violent deaths.* Westlake Village, CA: National School Safety Center.

U.S. Department of Education. (1998). *A guide to safe schools: Early warning, timely response.* Washington, DC: Author.

U.S. Department of Education. (1999). *Annual report on school safety 1998.* Washington, DC: Author.

6

Creating Positive Behavior Support Plans for Students With Significant Behavioral Challenges

Barbara J. Ayres
Montana State University–Billings

Deborah L. Hedeen
Idaho State University

Today's schools must address the behavioral needs of all students at a number of different levels. First, there must be schoolwide efforts that teach positive communication and social interaction skills, and develop positive school routines designed to prevent behavioral issues throughout the school day (Fishbaugh & Furshong, 1998; Scott, 2001; Taylor-Greene et al., 1997). Second, in conjunction with schoolwide efforts, classroom norms and routines can be established by educators, in collaboration with their students, to create a sense of caring and community in the classroom (Jones & Jones, 2001; Kohn, 1996; Sapon-Shevin, 1999). Third, behavioral issues must be addressed at the individual student level for students who have more intense, ongoing behavioral challenges (Hedeen, Ayres, Meyer, & Waite, 1996; Koegel, Koegel, & Dunlap, 1996; Scotti & Meyer, 1999). Addressing issues of school safety at the individual student level takes place through the creation of positive behavior support plans (Hedeen, Ayres, & Tate, 2001; Janney, Black, & Ferlo, 1989; Janney & Snell, 2000; O'Neill et al., 1997; Topper, Williams, Leo, Hamilton, & Fox, 1994).

When an individual student presents behavioral challenges, administrators and educators often fear for the safety of others in the school setting.

Their first reaction can be to respond to the student's behavior through the use of punishment and exclusion when what the student needs is to learn new skills and have stronger connections to the people around him or her. The process of creating a positive behavior support plan can help ensure that the issue of school safety is considered and addressed in a thoughtful, growth-oriented manner.

In a book edited by Koegel et al., (1996), positive behavioral support is defined as follows:

> [It is] the broad enterprise of helping people develop and engage in adaptive, socially desirable behaviors and overcome patterns of destructive and stigmatizing responding. The term typically refers to assistance that is provided for people with developmental, cognitive, or emotional/behavioral disabilities; however, the principles and approaches have much greater generality. Positive behavioral support incorporates a comprehensive set of procedures and support strategies that are selectively employed on the basis of an individual's needs, characteristics, and preferences. (p. xiii)

The purpose of this chapter is to describe a process for addressing the individual needs of students with challenging behaviors through the creation of positive behavior support plans. The important elements of positive behavioral supports are presented along with a case example and a sample positive behavior support plan.

JOSH[1]

Josh is a first-grade student who loves to use the computer and spend time with his friends. He likes to be involved in hands-on activities and is most successful when he is given a number of choices about his participation. He has a wonderful sense of humor and enjoys playing games with his peers. Josh has always had a strong desire to help others, both students and adults. Josh is difficult to understand when he speaks, but he can make his needs and desires known through the use of some words, his tone of voice, and pointing and showing others what he wants. In Josh's school file he is labeled as having a developmental disability.

Toward the end of his kindergarten year, Josh began having a great deal of difficulty making transitions from one activity to the next. For example, when he was playing on the computer and was told that it was time to stop, he would start pushing on the computer equipment, throwing the mouse and pad, kicking the computer table, screaming loudly, and grabbing for and kicking the adult who was next to him at the time. In the classroom when told that it was time to stop one activity and start another, Josh would fall to the floor and roll, kick, and scream. Though his actions were directed

---

[1] The case example of Josh is taken from an article written by the authors and previously published in the *Rural Special Education Quarterly* (Ayres & Hedeen, 1998).

at the teachers and paraeducators who provided his support, Josh was engaging in these behaviors in close proximity to his classmates, a major concern for the principal, teachers, and paraeducators in the building. Because adults had been hurt while working with Josh, their safety was also critical to his inclusion in the general-education classroom. The challenge facing the people involved in Josh's education was to create a plan that would prevent problems whenever possible while teaching Josh the new skills he needed to learn to be successful in the school environment. The following paragraphs describe key elements of positive behavioral supports and the steps that were taken to create a positive behavior support plan for Josh.

CREATING A POSITIVE BEHAVIOR SUPPORT PLAN

There are several key elements in the problem-solving process used to create a positive behavior support plan for an individual student (Janney & Snell, 2000; Topper et al., 1994). These include the following:

- Establish a collaborative team.
- Consider the posture of the adults who support the child.
- Determine the student's strengths and learning style.
- Identify the function of the behavior.
- Outline strategies that will prevent the behavior from occurring.
- Teach the student new skills to replace the challenging behavior.
- Respond to difficult behaviors in positive, supportive ways.

Each of these key elements is described in the subsections that follow as it relates to the creation of a positive behavior support plan for Josh. An example of his completed plan is provided in Table 6.1.

Establish a Collaborative Problem-Solving Team

To create schools that welcome, educate, and support all students, a team approach is crucial. Accommodating the needs of students with behavioral challenges is not the work of one person, but requires the collaborative effort of people who are involved in the student's life at home, school, and in the community. Sailor (1996) wrote, "The proverb 'it takes a whole village to raise a child' was never truer than when applied to a child who has severe behavior disorders" (p. 164). Collaborative problem-solving teams may include the student, parents/caregivers, extended family members, general- and special-education teachers, classmates, school administrators, paraeducators, speech pathologists, occupational and/or physical therapists, school psychologists, and school counselors. Though each collaborative team will include different members, it is essential that the individuals are

TABLE 6.1

Sample Behavior Support Plan

Behavior Support Plan

Student Name: Josh

Grade/Class: First Grade

Student's Strengths		**Team Members:**	
• Likes to be with others	• Likes to make choices	• Mother	• Special Ed Teacher
• Enjoys active learning	• Responds to visual cues & models	• Father	• AM Paraeducator
• Likes to help	• Good sense of humor	• Principal	• PM Paraeducator
• Excellent computer skills	• Enjoys games	• First Grade Teacher	

Challenging Behavior:	**Prevention Strategies:**	**New Skills to Replace Challenging Behavior:**	**Response When Behavior Occurs:**
• Crying, screaming, throwing objects, kicking	• Let Josh help during activities	• Teach Josh to make choices throughout the day	• Make participation as simple as possible
	• Give chores/jobs he can complete with peer	• Teach Josh to create daily schedule when he arrives at school	• Provide positive feedback as Josh attempts to participate
Communication of Behavior	• Have Josh work with peers during structured and unstructured activities	• Teach Josh to refer to picture/word schedule and note when he has completed a task	• Provide choices
• Need for predictability throughout the day	• Role playing with entire class—how to get attention, ask for help, take a break		• Take the activity to Josh to get him started (if he has left his desk)
• Need to feel a sense of control over daily activities	• Give lots of positive feedback	**Other Relevant Skills:**	• Looks for signs that Josh is become upset/anxious and cue him to request a break by pointing to card on desk.
	• Be organized and prepared for activities	• Increase expressive communication skills	
	• Provide written step-by-step directions for tasks	• Teach Josh to follow written step-by-step directions	
	• Communicate length of task	• Increase turn taking with peers	

Note. From Ayres, B. J., & Hedeen, D. L. (1998). Creating positive behavior support plans for students with significant behavioral challenges. *Rural Special Education Quarterly,* 17(3/4), 27–35. Reprinted by permission.

knowledgeable about and directly involved with the student (Anderson, Russo, Dunlap, & Albin, 1996; Thousand & Villa, 1990, 2000).

Josh's collaborative problem-solving team included his parents, the first-grade teacher, the special-education teacher, the paraeducators who worked with him throughout the day, and the building principal. Other individuals joined the team on an as-needed basis (e.g., the receiving teacher for the following year, speech pathologist, and school psychologist). The collaborative team met on a weekly basis to create and modify Josh's positive behavior support plan. Through creative scheduling during the day and after-school meetings, the school personnel and Josh's parents were able to join together and brainstorm ideas for Josh's plan.

Understand Adult Postures and How They Affect the Creation of Positive Behavioral Supports

A chapter written by McGee, Menousek, and Hobbs (1987) presented the idea of "posture" or the values and beliefs people hold, and the importance of understanding "our posture toward ourselves and others" when we are working to support individuals with challenging behaviors (p. 152). Four postures presented in this chapter include the following: cold/distancing, dependency-provoking/overprotective, authoritarian, and a posture of solidarity (see also McGee & Menolascino, 1991). In a similar discussion, Topper and her colleagues (1994) described "teaching styles which support preventing challenging behaviors" (p. 69) and used the terms *apathetic, permissive, authoritarian,* and *democratic.*

Regardless of the terms used to describe these postures, it is important to acknowledge that the attitudes held by the adults involved with a student will greatly influence the process of creating positive behavioral supports (Hedeen et al., 1996). For example, a classroom teacher with an authoritarian posture feels responsible for maintaining control and reacts to "misbehavior" primarily through correction and negative consequences. This person will feel that the student "knows better" and must be made accountable for his or her actions. A paraeducator with an overprotective/permissive posture will strive to keep the student from becoming upset, whatever the cost, in an attempt to not "rock the boat." A special-education teacher with a cold-mechanistic/apathetic posture will rely on dispensing consequences in a detached manner so as to avoid personal responsibility for the child's behavior. Finally, a school counselor with a democratic/solidarity posture will be interested in creating win/win situations for the adult and student. This person is more focused on developing a positive relationship with the student and preventing problems whenever possible while teaching new skills to replace the challenging behaviors. Problem solving and negotiation are crucial to this posture as is creating interdependence among people.

Creating a positive behavior support plan for an individual student with challenging behaviors requires team members to engage in thinking that embodies the democratic/solidarity posture. Unfortunately, this is not the predominant posture in our society where we assume that students are "choosing" to misbehave, know better, and should be punished for their actions (Kohn, 1996). Maag (2001) wrote, "there is a prevailing view that teachers' primary responsibility is to teach students academic behaviors and to control (i.e., bring into alignment) their socially inappropriate behaviors" (p. 182). He and other authors have written about how a difficult academic task such as reading or math would be analyzed by the teacher and restructured to create a successful experience for the student (Jones & Jones, 2001; Kohn, 1996; Maag, 2001). Yet behaviors such as speaking out of turn or leaving one's desk without permission would probably be followed by a negative consequence in an effort to decrease the behavior. Until we are willing to see difficult behaviors as an indication of a learning need, we will continue to struggle with our efforts to educate students who have behavioral issues. It is challenging for educators and others to analyze their posture and begin to make changes that move them toward a posture of solidarity with all of their students, including those who have challenges of behavior and learning.

In an article that focuses on the change process with regard to positive behavioral supports for individual students, Knoster and colleagues (2000) outlined specific enablers and inhibitors. They stated that one factor that can be an enabler if it is present and an inhibitor if not, is that "there must usually be an initial internal champion and/or external facilitator" (p. 24). They went on to say that "follow through and implementation can be compromised when there is no internal champion who understands the process and philosophy" (p. 24). This information is important to take into consideration for the creation and implementation of Josh's behavior support plan.

Josh's support team, though made up of a number of "internal champions"—people who truly believed in his inclusion and his potential for positive change, did require an external facilitator to support their efforts. A person with experience in positive behavioral supports was hired to provide ongoing child-centered consultation that included working directly with Josh and his teachers and paraeducators to model positive practices, videotape work sessions, and meet with the team to critique the videotapes and discuss their progress. The values and skills described and taught by the consultant allowed the members of Josh's team to change their posture over time. For example, one paraeducator who was initially very authoritarian with Josh (e.g., giving ultimatums, placing him in time-out, using excessive physical assistance to "force" participation), learned to be more proactive in her teaching by preventing problems whenever possible, defusing behaviors when they did occur, and redirecting Josh to the task at hand and enthusiastically praising his participation.

Determine the Student's Strengths and Learning Style

When creating a positive behavior support plan, the team can begin by identifying and building on the student's strengths and successes rather than focusing on the student's deficit areas (Brendtro & Brokenleg, 1993; Topper et al., 1994). Careful observation of the student, along with the synthesis of information gathered from all team members about when the student is most successful, provides important information for the support plan. A tool developed by Hobbs (1996) entitled, "In Search of a Person's Learning Style: Places to Begin Your Search" asks for information about the person in five categories: social interaction, participation, communication, emotional disposition, and use of body. Another useful tool, created by Armstrong (2000), entitled "Checklist for Assessing Students' Multiple Intelligences" provides insight on the individual's style in the areas of linguistic, logical-mathematical, spatial, bodily-kinesthetic, musical, interpersonal, and intrapersonal intelligences. With this information the team can create a learning style profile that contains invaluable information for the student's positive behavior support plan.

As they considered strengths and areas of success, Josh's team recognized that they had considerable information on his learning style that could be incorporated into the positive behavior support plan. They noted Josh's desire to interact with peers and help others, his love of the computer, his active participation in hands-on activities, and his interest in making choices and feeling a sense of control over the day's events. Acknowledging these strengths provided initial direction for the support plan (see Table 6.2). For example, the team considered why Josh was so successful when using the computer and decided that it could be that he enjoyed the predictability of the games and valued the step-by-step process that was used to start and to play the computer game. So, the next step in problem solving was to consider how predictability and step-by-step directions could be provided in other activities (and to determine ways to help Josh learn to transition successfully from the computer to the next activity). As the team learned more about Josh's successes they used this information to create the behavior support plan. In this way the plan focused on increasing positive options, versus simply addressing deficits. Table 6.1 illustrates how information on Josh's strengths was included in the positive behavior support plan.

Identify the Function of the Behavior

There is growing awareness and acceptance that behavior serves a communicative or self-regulatory purpose (Carr et al., 1994, Evans & Meyer, 1985; Janney & Snell, 2000; Topper et al., 1994). Often, individuals who are unable to communicate their feelings and needs effectively will use behaviors to tell others they want attention, need to avoid a difficult situation, or require

TABLE 6.2

Considering Josh's Learning Style
When Creating the Positive Behavior Support Plan

If ...	Then ...
likes interaction	include peers in lessons
difficulty getting started w/ new activities	give warnings/build interest
throws materials	control/limit materials
finishes work quickly	give smaller amounts
likes to help	give jobs/errands
bored, detached, sad	be enthusiastic
difficulty expressing needs	use picture symbols
trouble processing verbal information	use picture symbols
dislikes physical contact	give physical space
slow moving	give time to respond
likes to sit/lie down	use chair/beanbag
likes predictable sequences	lay out steps of activities

a sense of control. At other times the behaviors may serve a play function or meet the person's need for self-regulation. In addition to the team's observations and insights there are a number of tools that can be used to create hypotheses for the function of the behavior (Donnellan, Mirenda, Mesaros, & Fassbender, 1984; Durand, 1988; Lewis, Scott, & Sugai, 1994).

Though determining the function of the behavior is not new to the field of behavioral intervention (Carr & Durand, 1985; Durand, 1990), it does require that team members have a certain posture toward the student and his or her behavior. It is difficult for an adult, who feels that the student knows better and should be punished for his or her actions, to engage in a discussion on the function behind the behavior. Once people understand and internalize this thinking, however, great strides can be made in creating truly positive supports for the individual. For example, in a first-grade class that included a child with challenging behaviors, the students were encouraged to write about their classmate toward the end of the school year. One girl wrote the following comments in her own handwriting and with her own spelling:

> At the beginning of the year Will's screams were just screams to us. But now, we can tell if they mean frusteration, happiness, sadness, fright, or if he just wants us to leave him alone. It might be nice if Will could write an autobiography about his life. That would make it more interesting. Sometimes we have to change some activities so he can partisapate. But, however he lives, however he talks to us, he is still one of us.

This first-grade student's understanding of the function of behavior gives us hope that over time, more adults will be able to engage in the same kind of thinking.

In considering the function of the behavior, we are asked to understand that there is nothing wrong with what the person is trying to accomplish through his or her behavior, but that he or she might need to learn a more "acceptable" way to communicate the same message. Topper and her colleagues (1994) went a step further in the discussion of behavioral function to identify positive aspects of the behaviors we are working to address. For example, when a student is using a behavior to get attention from others we could consider that relationships with others are important to the student. When a student uses behaviors to gain a sense of control, we could interpret it as the student demonstrating his or her leadership potential.

When Josh's team met to consider the function behind his behaviors of crying, screaming, throwing objects, and kicking, they hypothesized that he might be trying to communicate his need for predictability and a sense of control over the situation. Many of the behaviors occurred when it was time to transition from one activity to the next and his behaviors might have indicated that he was not sure why he had to stop, what he was going to do next, and when he could again gain access to a preferred activity. Josh's team hypothesized that his behaviors served the function of gaining control over daily events. Table 6.1 includes information on the function of the behavior as a part of the positive behavior support plan.

Once the function of the behavior is determined, the team can begin to think about how to use this information to create the behavior support plan. This plan will include strategies for prevention of problems, new skills to replace the challenging behavior, and how to respond to difficult situations with supportive, educational responses.

Determine Prevention Strategies

A critical component of a positive behavior support plan is the selection of strategies that will prevent the challenging behavior from occurring. Too often we wait until the behavior has taken place and then try to determine our response. This kind of "reactive" teaching allows the student to continue practicing the challenging behavior. A more effective approach is to be "proactive" and prevent problems as we teach new, more acceptable skills that can replace the challenging behavior.

In determining prevention strategies the team should consider the following options: (a) increasing the choices provided to the student and creating a sense of control, (b) increasing opportunities for positive attention throughout the day, (c) increasing the student's status in the classroom and school, (d) developing the student's positive self-image, (e) matching strategies and activities with the student's strengths, and (f) matching the physical arrangement of the classroom to the student's needs (Topper et al., 1994). These six options fit into a framework that includes changing the physical, instructional, and social environment (see Table 6.3). In addition, Janney and Snell (2000) presented many ideas for prevention that are framed around three categories: who, what, and when.

In determining prevention strategies for Josh, the team selected a number of ideas that addressed the aforementioned six points and meshed both with his strengths and with the function of the behavior (see Table 6.1). For example, the team recognized Josh's desire to help others and interact with his peers. They combined this information with his need to feel a sense of predictability and control, and selected the strategy of providing Josh with many opportunities throughout his day to perform errands for the teacher and jobs in the classroom with a peer he selected. This strategy addressed the options listed earlier by increasing the opportunities for choice making and increasing Josh's status and self-image. To address Josh's difficulties with transitioning from one activity to the next, the team decided that he needed to have tasks carefully organized and defined. For example, the adult working with Josh needed to have all the materials ready before starting an activity and clearly show him how long they would work on that particular activity. Josh also needed to know what was coming next after he completed the activity. The team found that Josh was most successful when he used a picture schedule that delineated the day's activities. Once again, these strategies meshed his strengths and needs and addressed two of the options for prevention strategies: matching strategies with strengths, and increasing choices to create a sense of control.

Teach New Skills to Replace the Challenging Behavior

With the growing acceptance that behaviors serve a purpose for the student, educators and parents also acknowledge that new, positive communication and social interaction skills must be taught to replace the challenging behavior (Evans & Meyer, 1985; Wolery & Winterling, 1997). For example, if a child grabs the clothing of other students on the playground, and we feel that she is using this behavior to communicate her desire for attention, we must replace the grabbing behavior with a more acceptable way to get attention such as tapping her classmates on the shoulder and asking if they want to play. If a student throws materials off his desk after attempting to complete a task, and we hypothesize that he is trying to communicate that he is frustrated and needs to escape the situation, we would replace the throwing behavior with teaching the student to ask for a break when he starts to feel frustrated. In this way asking for a break replaces throwing the materials off the desk (see Table 6.3). It is important to understand the function of the behavior and then select a replacement skill that will meet the same need. In other words, the message is a good one to

TABLE 6.3
Developing a Positive Behavior Support Plan

PREVENT	TEACH	RESPOND
The most effective way to address difficult behaviors is to prevent them from occurring. This can be accomplished by changing the physical, instructional, and/or social environment.	Teaching new skills involves determining what the student needs to learn to replace the challenging behavior. Therefore, it is necessary to understand the purpose of the behavior so that a replacement skill can be selected.	A positive behavior support plan emphasizes prevention and teaching versus focusing primarily on how to "react" once the behavior has occurred. It is important, however, to plan for the occurrence of behaviors so that everyone is prepared and confident in how to respond. The following strategies are suggested as ways to respond that can defuse difficult situations.
1) Change the **Physical Environment** • Rearrange furniture or materials • Work at different locations in classroom • Remove items that make participation or transitions difficult • Seat students for safety and participation	1) Student grabs classmate at recess. Purpose: To get classmate's **attention**. <u>Teach</u> the student to tap classmate on shoulder.	• Watch for signs/precursors to the behavior and make changes to prevent additional problems • Provide choices of materials/activities • Take a short break • Remain calm • Take materials to the student • Say nothing about the behavior while you continue to teach, focusing on participation
2) Adapt the **Instructional Environment** • Change the difficulty, amount, or sequence or work • Use visual strategies to assist with steps of tasks • Include manipulatives and movement within the lesson	2) Student throws materials off desk. Purpose: To **escape/avoid** difficult work. <u>Teach</u> student to raise hand for help or take work to adult.	
	3) Student runs out of the classroom. Purpose: To **get something**—a drink of water. <u>Teach</u> student to give picture symbol of water fountain to adult.	

(continued on next page)

TABLE 6.3 (*continued*)

PREVENT	TEACH	RESPOND
3) Change the **Social Environment** • Alternate people in routines • Teach classmates how to interact successfully with student • Provide choices throughout the day • Increase opportunities for positive attention from adults and peers • Give the student valued roles and responsibilities These changes can prevent the behavior from occurring so that the student will experience successful interaction and participation. Through preventative efforts, our attention is focused on creating a positive learning environment versus waiting for the behavior to occur and then responding.	4) Student takes items from teacher's desk. Purpose: To **play** with objects. <u>Teach</u> student to select an item from personal belongings to play with during free time. 5) Student leaves desk a few times during lesson to jump or clap hands. Purpose: To **self-regulate** and release tension. <u>Teach</u> student to go to back of room to engage in activities designed to release tension and reduce stress.	• Redirect the person to the task through nonverbal cues and physical assistance • Make participation errorless • Provide positive feedback for any attempts to participate • Be enthusiastic • Use predictable materials/activities • Compromise/adjust plan • Protect yourself and others in a nonintrusive manner The use of punishment or other intrusive interventions is not the solution to addressing challenging behaviors. We must acknowledge that behaviors serve a purpose for the person and are an indication of a learning need. We can then use our best teaching strategies to help the person learn new communication, social, and self-regulatory behaviors.

communicate, but the way to communicate it needs to be actively addressed through teaching new skills.

Because Josh's team felt that his behavior was communicating his need for predictability and control, they selected the replacement skills of making choices and using a picture/word schedule (see Table 6.1). They actively taught these skills throughout the day. For example, they infused making choices into every activity by providing opportunities for Josh to choose which writing utensil and paper he would use for assignments, where he wanted to sit in the room to complete an activity, which peer he would like to work with on the computer, and what activity he would like to engage in during free time in the classroom. They provided choices in the form of actual objects or line drawings of objects and activities. With regard to using the picture/word schedule, Josh had many opportunities to refer to the schedule throughout the day. When he arrived each morning, Josh put his daily schedule together with assistance from the paraeducator, noting any changes in activities or people. They talked through his day and the paraeducator shared information with Josh that would help him become excited about, connect to, and anticipate certain activities. Throughout the day as Josh completed an activity he would refer back to the schedule, turn over the picture of the activity he had just completed, and point to and discuss the upcoming activity.

Respond to Behavioral Challenges in Supportive Ways

When using positive behavioral supports, our emphasis changes from increasing and decreasing behaviors through consequences to a focus on prevention and teaching new skills. If we accept the notion that behavior serves a function and is an indication of a learning need, it stands to reason that we would begin to think about responding to behavioral challenges in new ways. As we learn more about the student and his or her behaviors, and are able to prevent problems from occurring in the first place while we actively teach new skills to replace the challenging behaviors, we find ourselves responding to difficult situations much less frequently. When we need to respond, we can remain supportive versus resorting to the use of punishment (see Table 6.3). Some strategies that are useful when a person is struggling include offering choices, getting the student involved in the task at hand, allowing the student to take a break to regain composure, and providing positive attention for any attempts the student makes to interact and participate (McGee et al., 1987; Topper et al., 1994). It is important that everyone is safe during a challenging situation and that everyone respects the dignity of all involved.

Additional problem solving can occur after a challenging situation when the adults reflect on how the problem could have been prevented and what they will do differently the next time. Peers can also engage in the problem-solving process and often provide wonderful insights that have escaped the adults. Their active involvement is often crucial to the success of the strategies included in the positive behavior support plan.

When Josh was in first grade the behaviors of rolling on the floor, screaming, throwing objects, kicking, and hitting were serious. He met most transitions from one activity to the next with these behaviors. His team worked hard to implement the prevention and teaching strategies identified in the previous sections. As Josh was prepared for activities, shown his picture schedule, and given increased positive attention for his participation, his difficult behaviors decreased over time. In the beginning, however, there were times when Josh would use the behaviors described previously that had been a part of his routine for at least 2 years. During these times the adults providing his support worked to remain positive and supportive (see Table 6.1). Often, if the adults provided Josh with a choice as he started becoming upset, he would respond positively and continue with the task. At other times the adult neutralized the behavior by not attending to it while refocusing Josh on the task, making his participation as easy as possible, and rewarding his efforts. There were also situations where Josh's behaviors were escalating and the best response was to suggest a break from the classroom. The adult providing his support assisted him to indicate that he needed a break and to leave the room for a walk, to get a drink, or to run an errand for the teacher. These breaks were used as a way to keep Josh's behavior from escalating to the point where someone could get hurt. This also allowed Josh's classmates to remain calm and focused. Over time, as the team implemented the ideas generated through their collaborative efforts, Josh's challenging behaviors of kicking, screaming, hitting, and throwing decreased as he learned to use the new skills of making choices and referring to the picture/word schedule throughout his day.

CONCLUSION

Schools at the turn of the 21st century are asked to welcome and educate a very diverse group of students. Effective schools are finding that they need to address issues of behavior at three levels: schoolwide, classwide, and at the individual student level. Educators are moving toward a posture that allows them to teach to behavioral issues versus react to them. These efforts require educators to work collaboratively with home and community, engage in a discussion of the function of the behavior, and create plans that involve strategies for preventing problems, teaching new skills, and responding in positive, supportive ways. One student will not negatively affect school safety when we create, implement, and evaluate positive behavior support plans through active collaboration and teaching.

By the way, one of the authors saw Josh the other day and he is now a fourth grader. He was playing a computer game and when it was time to quit he "shut down" the program (with no advance warning), stood up, and pushed in his chair. When congratulated on how well he left the computer and reminded of his struggles years ago, he just smiled enthusiastically and gave the author "five." Despite the challenges faced a few years ago by Josh's team and the greater school community, he was not excluded. A plan was created that connected Josh to his educators and peers in ways that will affect them all for a lifetime.

CHAPTER ACTIVITIES

For Discussion

1.   How could you go about creating a team that would support a student with challenging behaviors in the school setting?

2.   Why is it important to determine a student's learning style when creating a positive behavior support plan? How can this information be used by the team?

3.   How could you engage the team members in a discussion about the function of the student's behavior, especially if they felt that the student "knew better" and was choosing to act in a certain way? Why is understanding the function of the behavior an important element of positive behavioral supports?

4.   Discuss the three key components of a positive behavior support plan: preventing problems, teaching new skills, and responding in supportive ways. If the team were focusing on consequences and reacting to behaviors after they have occurred, how could you move the discussion toward the importance of prevention and teaching new skills?

Case Study

Work with a partner or small group to describe a student you know who has "challenged the system." Follow the process described in this chapter to create a positive behavior support plan for the student.

1. Who would be on the support team?
2. Discuss the posture of the adults who are supporting the student.
3. Determine the student's strengths and learning style.
4. Describe the student's behavior in observable and measurable terms and hypothesize about the function of the behavior.
5. Outline strategies that could prevent the behavior from occurring.
6. Discuss what new skills the student needs to learn to replace the challenging behavior. Describe how you will go about teaching these new skills.

7. Brainstorm ideas for responding to the behavior in ways that are nonpunitive, positive, and educational.

REFERENCES

Anderson, J. L., Russo, A., Dunlap, G., & Albin, R. W. (1996). A team training model for building the capacity to provide positive behavioral supports in inclusive settings. In L. K. Koegel, R. L. Koegel, & G. Dunlap (Eds.), *Positive behavioral support* (pp. 467–490). Baltimore: Paul H. Brookes.

Armstrong, T. (2000). *Multiple intelligences in the classroom* (2nd ed.). Alexandria, VA: Association for Supervision and Curriculum Development.

Ayres, B. J., & Hedeen, D. L. (1998). Creating positive behavior support plans for students with significant behavioral challenges. *Rural Special Education Quarterly* 17(3/4), 27–35.

Brendtro, L. K., & Brokenleg, M. (1993). Beyond the curriculum of control. *The Journal of Emotional & Behavioral Problems, 1*(4), 5–11.

Carr, E. G., & Durand, V. M. (1985). Reducing behavior problems through functional communication training. *Journal of Applied Behavior Analysis, 18,* 111–126.

Carr, E. G., Levin, L., McConnachie, G., Carlson, J. I., Kemp, D. C., & Smith, C. E. (1994). *Communication-based intervention for problem behavior.* Baltimore: Paul H. Brookes.

Donnellan, A. M., Mirenda, P. L., Mesaros, R. A., & Fassbender, L. L. (1984). Analyzing the communicative functions of aberrant behavior. *Journal of the Association for Persons with Severe Handicaps, 9,* 201–212.

Durand, V. M. (1988). The Motivation Assessment Scale. In M. Hersen & A. S. Bellack (Eds.), *Dictionary of behavioral assessment techniques* (pp. 309–310). New York: Pergamon.

Durand, V. M. (1990). *Severe behavior problems: A functional communication training approach.* New York: Guilford.

Evans, I. M., & Meyer, L. H. (1985). *An educative approach to behavior problems.* Baltimore: Paul H. Brookes.

Fishbaugh, M. S. E., & Furshong, J. (1998). The Montana Behavioral Initiative: A statewide response. *Rural Special Education Quarterly, 17*(3/4), 48–61.

Hedeen, D. L., Ayres, B. J., Meyer, L. H., & Waite, J. (1996). Quality inclusive schooling for students with severe behavioral challenges. In D. H. Lehr & F. Brown (Eds.), *People with disabilities who challenge the system* (pp. 127–171). Baltimore: Paul H. Brookes.

Hedeen, D. L., Ayres, B. J., & Tate, A. (2001). Charlotte's story: Getting better, happy day, problems again! In M. Grenot-Scheyer, M. Fisher, & D. Staub (Eds.), *At the end of the day: Lessons learned in inclusive education* (pp. 47–72). Baltimore: Paul H. Brookes.

Hobbs, D. (1996). *In search of a person's learning style: Places to begin your search.* Springfield, NE: Hobbs Training and Support Services.

Janney, R., Black, J., & Ferlo, M. (1989). *A problem-solving approach to challenging behaviors.* Syracuse, NY: Syracuse University, Special Projects.

Janney, R., & Snell, M. E. (2000). *Teachers' guides to inclusive practices: Behavioral support.* Baltimore: Paul H. Brookes.

Jones, V. F., & Jones, L. S. (2001). *Comprehensive classroom management: Creating communities of support and solving problems* (6th ed.). Boston: Allyn & Bacon.

Knoster, T., Kincaid, D., Brinkley, J., Malatchi, A., McFarland, J., Shannon, P., Hazelgrove, J., & Schall, C. (2000). Insights on implementing positive behavior support in schools. *TASH Newsletter, 26*(10), 23–25.

Koegel, L. K., Koegel, R. L., & Dunlap, G. (1996). *Positive behavioral support.* Baltimore: Paul H. Brookes.

Kohn, A. (1996). *Beyond discipline: From compliance to community.* Alexandria, VA: Association for Supervision and Curriculum Development.

Lewis, T. J., Scott, T., & Sugai, G. (1994). The problem behavior questionnaire: A teacher based instrument to develop functional hypotheses of problem behavior in general education classrooms. *Diagnostique, 19,* 103–115.

Maag, J. W. (2001). Rewarded by punishment: Reflections on the disuse of positive reinforcement in schools. *Exceptional Children, 67*(2), 173–186.

McGee, J., & Menolascino, F. (1991). *Beyond gentle teaching.* New York: Plenum.

McGee, J., Menousek, P., & Hobbs, D. (1987). Gentle teaching: An alternative to punishment for people with challenging behaviors. In S. J. Taylor, D. Biklen, & J. Knoll (Eds.), *Community integration for people with severe disabilities* (pp. 147–183). New York: Teachers College Press.

O'Neill, R. E., Horner, R. H., Albin, R. W., Sprague, J. R., Storey, K., & Newton, J. S. (1997). *Functional assessment and program development for problem behavior.* Pacific Grove, CA: Brooks/Cole.

Sailor, W. (1996). New structures and systems change for comprehensive positive behavioral support. In L. K. Koegel, R. L. Koegel, & G. Dunlap (Eds.), *Positive behavioral support* (pp. 163–206). Baltimore: Paul H. Brookes.

Sapon-Shevin, M. (1999). *Because we can change the world.* Boston: Allyn & Bacon.

Scott, T. M. (2001). A schoolwide example of positive behavioral support. *Journal of Positive Behavior Interventions, 3*(2), 88–94.

Scotti, J. R., & Meyer, L. H. (1999). *Behavioral intervention: Principles, models, and practices.* Baltimore: Paul H. Brookes.

Taylor-Greene, S., Brown, D., Nelson, L., Longton, J., Gassman, T., Cohen, J., Swartz, J., Horner, R., Sugai, G., & Hall, S. (1997). Schoolwide behavioral support: Starting the year off right. *Journal of Behavioral Education, 7*(1), 99–112.

Thousand, J. S., & Villa, R. A. (1990). Sharing expertise and responsibilities through teaching teams. In W. Stainback & S. Stainback (Eds.), *Support networks for inclusive schooling: Interdependent integrated education* (pp. 123–138). Baltimore: Paul H. Brookes.

Thousand, J. S., & Villa, R. A. (2000). Collaborative teaming: A powerful tool in school restructuring. In R. A. Villa & J. S. Thousand (Eds.), *Restructuring for caring and effective education* (pp. 254–291). Baltimore: Paul H. Brookes.

Topper, K., Williams, W., Leo, K., Hamilton, R., & Fox, T. (1994). *A positive approach to understanding and addressing challenging behaviors.* Burlington: University of Vermont, Center for Developmental Disabilities.

Wolery, M., & Winterling, V. (1997). Curricular approaches to controlling severe behavior problems. In N. N. Singh (Ed.), *Prevention and treatment of severe behavior problems* (pp. 87–120). Pacific Grove, CA: Brooks/Cole.

7

School–Community Relations: Policy and Practice

Linda Taylor

Howard S. Adelman
Center for Mental Health in Schools, UCLA

School personnel long have understood that if schools are to function well and students are to learn effectively, factors that interfere with students' learning and performance must be addressed. Some efforts have been made to do so. These include reforms designed to enhance school–community relations. Effective school–community connections have the potential to expand opportunities for improving the quality of youngsters' lives and their expectations for a positive future by addressing barriers to learning and promoting healthy development.

The litany of barriers to learning is all too familiar to anyone who works with students in schools. Too often, available resources are insufficient to the task of providing basic developmental and learning opportunities. Thus, youngsters bring to school a variety of problems stemming from restricted opportunities associated with poverty, difficult and diverse family circumstances, poor language skills, inadequate health care, and more. How many are affected? Figures vary. Harold Hodgkinson (1989), Director of the Center for Demographic Policy, estimated that 40% of young people are in very bad educational shape and at risk of failing to fulfill their promise. Relatively few of these children start out with internal factors (psychological and/or biological) predisposing them to trouble. The majority end up having difficulties because they have experienced a range of external barriers that interfere with their succeeding at school (e.g., violence, drugs, frequent school changes, and a host of problems that confront recent immigrants and families living in poverty).

Ultimately, addressing barriers to learning must be approached from a social policy perspective. Fundamental systemic reforms are required that can improve practices for supporting and enabling learning. As discussed in this chapter, a major facet of all this is the development of a comprehensive, integrated continuum of community and school programs (Adelman, 1996b; Schorr, 1997).

ENHANCING SCHOOL–COMMUNITY CONNECTIONS TO ADDRESS BARRIERS TO STUDENT LEARNING

Initiatives to link community resources with each other and with schools are under way across the country. Along with such initiatives has come an increasing emphasis on establishing *collaboratives* involving school, home, and community as one way to provide more support for schools, students, and families (Adler & Gardner, 1994; Schorr, 1997). The interest in such collaboration is bolstered by the renewed concern for countering widespread fragmentation of school and community interventions (Dryfoos, 1994). The hope is that, by integrating available resources, a significant impact can be made on a myriad of "at risk" factors. There is much to learn from these efforts.

Various levels and forms of collaboration are being tested, including statewide initiatives in California, Florida, Kentucky, Missouri, New Jersey, Ohio, Oregon, and Utah among others. The aims are to improve coordination and eventually integrate many programs and enhance their linkages to school sites. To these ends, major demonstration projects across the country are incorporating as many health, mental health, and social services as feasible into "centers" (including school-based health centers, family and parent centers) established at or near a school. They adopt terms such as school-linked and coordinated services, wraparound, one-stop shopping, full-service schools, and community schools (Adelman, 1996a; Dryfoos, 1994). There are projects to (a) improve access to health services and access to social service programs, such as foster care, family preservation, child care; (b) expand after-school academic, recreation, and enrichment, such as tutoring, youth sports and clubs, art, music, museum programs; (c) build systems of care, such as case management and specialized assistance; (d) reduce delinquency (preventing drug abuse and truancy, providing conflict mediation and reducing violence); (e) enhance transitions to work/career/postsecondary education; and (f) enhance life in school and community, such as programs to adopt a school, use of volunteer and peer supports, and building neighborhood coalitions.

With respect to a host of concerns, then, there is considerable interest in developing strong relationships between school sites and public and private community agencies. Such interest meshes nicely with the renewed attention given to human service integration over the past 20 years. Major aims include reducing fragmentation of effort and, in the process, evolving better ways to meet needs and use existing resources.

Orientations to School—Community Initiatives

In analyzing school–community initiatives, Franklin and Streeter (1995) grouped them as informal, coordinated, partnerships, collaborations, and integrated services. These categories are seen as differing in terms of the degree of system change required. As would be anticipated, most initial efforts focus on developing informal relationships and beginning to coordinate services. The following are a few examples of different orientations to connecting schools and communities.

School-Linked Services.   With a view to improving access to and for clients, community agencies have developed the notion of school-linked services. A nationwide survey of school board members reported by Hardiman, Curcio, and Fortune (1998) indicates widespread presence of school-linked programs and services in school districts. For purposes of the survey, school-linked services were defined as "the coordinated linking of school and community resources to support the needs of school-aged children and their families" (p. 37). The researchers concluded that school-linked services are used in varying degrees to address many educational, psychological, health, and social concerns, including substance abuse, job training, teen pregnancy, juvenile probation, child and family welfare, and housing. Not surprisingly, the majority of schools report using school-linked resources as part of their efforts to deal with substance abuse; far fewer report such involvement with respect to family welfare and housing. Most of this activity reflects collaboration with agencies at local and state levels. Respondents indicate that these collaborations operate under a variety of arrangements: "legislative mandates, state-level task forces and commissions, formal agreements with other state agencies, formal and informal agreements with local government agencies, in-kind (nonmonetary) support of local government and nongovernment agencies, formal and informal referral network, and the school administrator's prerogative" (Hardiman et al., 1998, p. 38). About half the respondents note that their districts have no policies governing school-linked services.

In some instances, initiatives for school-linked services involve enough community agencies that they are described as "full-service schools." Communities that have developed "systems of care" also strive to encompass school programs and services in their wraparound efforts.

Youth Development Programs.   In addition to involvements related to school-linked services, schools are connecting, for example, with the growing youth development movement. This movement encompasses concepts and practices aimed at promoting protective factors, asset building, wellness, and empowerment. It embraces a wide range of stakeholders, including families and community-based and -linked organizations such as public and private health and human service agencies, schools, businesses, youth and faith organizations, and so forth. In some cases, institutions for postsecondary learning also are involved, but the nature and scope of their participation varies greatly, as does the motivation for the involvement. Youth development initiatives encourage a view of schools not only as community centers where families can easily access services, but also as hubs for community-wide learning and activity. Increased federal funding for after-school programs at school sites is enhancing this view by expanding opportunities for recreation, enrichment, academic supports, and child care (Larner, Zippiroli, & Behrman, 1999).

Strengthening Families and Neighborhoods.   Going beyond school-linked services and youth development, Schorr (1997) approached community–school initiatives from the perspective of strengthening families and neighborhoods. Based on her analysis of promising partnerships, she concluded that a synthesis is emerging that "rejects addressing poverty, welfare, employment, education, child development, housing, and crime one at a time. It endorses the idea that the multiple and interrelated problems ... require multiple and interrelated solutions" (p. 319).

Current Status of School–Community Initiatives

In surveying school–community initiatives, Melaville and Blank (1998) stated that the numbers are skyrocketing and the diversity in terms of design, management, and funding arrangements is dizzying and daunting. Their analysis led them to suggest (a) the initiatives are moving toward blended and integrated purposes and activity and (b) the activities are predominantly school based and the education sector plays "a significant role in the creation and, particularly, management of these initiatives" (p. 100) and there is a clear trend "toward much greater community involvement in all aspects" (p. 100) of such initiatives—especially in decision making at both the community and site levels. They also stressed that "the ability of school–community initiatives to strengthen school functioning develops incrementally" (p. 100), with the first impact seen in improved school climate.

Findings from our work (e.g., Center for Mental Health in Schools, 1996, 1997) are in considerable agreement with other reports. However, we also stress that the majority of school and community programs and services still function in relative isolation of each other. Most continue to focus on discrete problems and specialized services for individuals and small groups. Moreover, because the primary emphasis is on restructuring community programs and colocating some services on school sites, a new form of fragmentation is emerging as community and school professionals engage in a form of parallel play at school sites. Thus, ironically, whereas initiatives to integrate health and human services are meant to reduce fragmentation (with the intent of enhancing outcomes), in many cases fragmentation is compounded because these initiatives focus mostly on *linking community services to schools*. It appears that too little thought has been given to the importance of *connecting* community *programs* with existing programs operated by the school. As a result, when community agencies colocate personnel at schools, such personnel tend to operate in relative isolation of existing school programs and services. Little attention is paid to developing effective mechanisms for coordinating complementary activity or integrating parallel efforts. Consequently, a youngster identified as at risk for substance abuse, dropout, and suicide may be involved in three counseling programs operating independently of each other.

Based on the evidence to date, fragmentation is worsened by the failure of policymakers at all levels to recognize the need to reform and restructure the work of school and community professionals who are in positions to address barriers and promote development. Reformers mainly talk about "school-linked integrated services"—apparently in the belief that a few health and social services will do the trick. Such talk has led some policymakers to the mistaken impression that community resources alone can effectively meet the needs of schools in addressing barriers to learning. In turn, this has led some legislators to view linking community services to schools as a way to free up the dollars underwriting school-owned services. The reality is that even when one adds together community and school assets, the total set of services in impoverished locales is woefully inadequate. In situation after situation, it has become evident that as soon as the first few sites demonstrating school–community collaboration are in place, community agencies find they have stretched their resources to the limit. Another problem is that the overemphasis on school-linked services is exacerbating rising tensions between school district service personnel and their counterparts in community-based organizations. As "outside" professionals offer services at schools, school specialists often view the trend as discounting their skills and threatening their jobs. At the same time, the "outsiders" often feel unappreciated and may be rather naive about the culture of schools. Conflicts arise over "turf," use of space, confidentiality, and liability. Thus, collaboration still is not the norm.

In general, efforts to enhance school–community connections are based in policy initiatives that not only lack cohesiveness, but are formulated in an ad hoc manner that leads to piecemeal and fragmented practices. Not surprisingly, the fragmentation has worked against effectiveness.

More fundamentally, problems arise because prevailing approaches to school reform continue to *marginalize* all efforts designed to address barriers to student learning (Center for Mental Health in Schools, 1997). Marginalization in policy leads to marginalization in practice. The consequences are seen in the lack of attention given to addressing barriers to learning in consolidated plans and program quality reviews and the lack of efforts to map, analyze, and rethink resource allocation. The effects of marginalization also are seen in the ongoing disregard for the need to restructure what schools and communities already are doing to prevent and ameliorate youngsters' problems. This results in the continued failure to reframe the work of professionals whose job it is to deal with students' behavioral, learning, and emotional problems. All this tends to maintain the token way such matters are dealt with in preservice and continuing education for administrative and line staff. Given this state of affairs, it is not surprising how little is known about effective processes and mechanisms for building school–community connections to prevent and ameliorate young people's problems. Clearly, a great deal more work is needed on the problem of connecting the resources of schools, families, and communities.

Nevertheless, a reasonable inference from available data is that school–community collaborations can be successful and cost effective over the long run. They not only improve access to services, but they also seem to encourage schools to open their doors in ways that enhance recreational, enrichment, and remedial opportunities and family involvement.

Moving Beyond the Notion of School-Linked Services and Full Service Schools

Though not prescriptive, analyses of deficiencies related to current policy underscore the need for new directions and for bold thinking in formulating new directions. Inspiration can be found in emerging trends and innovative "big picture" analyses for enhancing the well-being of youngsters (Adelman & Taylor, 1993, 1997, 1998a, 2000; Dryfoos, 1998; Schorr, 1997).

For example, the growing youth development and community school movements clearly expand intervention efforts beyond services and programs. They often include a focus on ensuring that services are available. However, they also encompass (a) programs for community and social capital mobilization and (b) initiatives to build community policies and structures to enhance youth support, safety, recreation, work, service, and enrichment (Burt, 1998; Cahill, 1998; Catalano & Hawkins, 1995; Dryfoos, 1998; Schorr, 1997). In some cases, institutions for postsecondary learning also are involved, but the nature and scope of participation varies greatly. By moving beyond school-linked services, such initiatives encourage a view of schools not only as community centers where families can easily access services, but also as hubs for community-wide learning and activity. Increased federal funding for after-school programs at school sites is enhancing this view by expanding opportunities for recreation, enrichment, academic supports, and child care. Adult education and training at school sites also help change the old view that schools close when the youngsters leave. Indeed, the concept of a "second shift" at school sites is beginning to spread in communities across the country.

All this is moving in the right direction. However, even more comprehensive approaches are needed.

TOWARD COMPREHENSIVE, MULTIFACETED APPROACHES

Based on our understanding of prevailing initiatives and related efforts for addressing problems experienced by young people, we submit the following propositions. We suggest that many specific problems are best pursued as an integrated part of a comprehensive, multifaceted continuum of interventions designed to address barriers to learning and promote healthy development. For another, we submit that comprehensive, multifaceted approaches are feasible only if the resources of schools, families, and communities are woven together. A corollary of this is that the committed involvement of school, family, and community is essential in maximizing intervention implementation and effectiveness.

With these propositions firmly in mind, in this section we discuss two topics. Each represents a major arena for policy and practice to make the aforementioned propositions a reality. First, we place all initiatives for addressing barriers to learning within the context of a comprehensive and multifaceted continuum of braided interventions. Then, we explore the importance of thoroughly integrating such initiatives into prevailing school reforms.

A Comprehensive and Multifaceted Continuum of Braided Interventions

Problems experienced by students generally are complex in terms of cause and needed intervention. This means interventions must be comprehensive and multifaceted.

How comprehensive and multifaceted? As illustrated in Fig. 7.1, the desired interventions can be conceived as a continuum ranging from a broad-based emphasis on promoting healthy development and preventing problems (both of which include a focus on wellness or competence enhancement) through approaches for responding to problems early-after-onset, and extending on to narrowly focused treatments for severe/chronic problems. Not only does the continuum span the concepts of primary, secondary, and tertiary prevention, it can incorporate a holistic and developmental emphasis that envelops individuals, families, and the contexts in which they live, work, and play. The continuum also provides a framework for adhering to the principle of using the least restrictive and nonintrusive

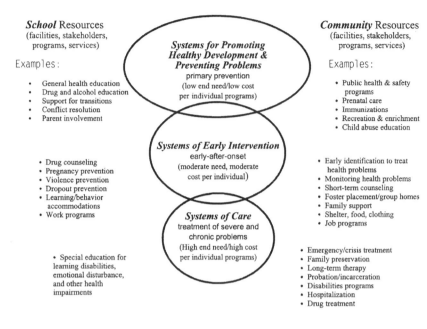

School Resources
(facilities, stakeholders,
programs, services)

Examples:

- General health education
- Drug and alcohol education
- Support for transitions
- Conflict resolution
- Parent involvement

- Drug counseling
- Pregnancy prevention
- Violence prevention
- Dropout prevention
- Learning/behavior
  accommodations
- Work programs

- Special education for
  learning disabilities,
  emotional disturbance,
  and other health
  impairments

Community Resources
(facilities, stakeholders,
programs, services)

Examples:

- Public health & safety
  programs
- Prenatal care
- Immunizations
- Recreation & enrichment
- Child abuse education

- Early identification to treat
  health problems
- Monitoring health problems
- Short-term counseling
- Foster placement/group homes
- Family support
- Shelter, food, clothing
- Job programs

- Emergency/crisis treatment
- Family preservation
- Long-term therapy
- Probation/incarceration
- Disabilities programs
- Hospitalization
- Drug treatment

Systems for Promoting Healthy Development & Preventing Problems
primary prevention
(low end need/low cost
per individual programs)

Systems of Early Intervention
early-after-onset
(moderate need, moderate
cost per individual)

Systems of Care
treatment of severe and
chronic problems
(High end need/high cost
per individual programs)

Systemic collaboration* is essential to establish interprogram connections on a daily basis and over time to ensure seamless intervention within each system and among *systems* of *prevention, systems* of *early intervention,* and *systems of care.*

*Such collaboration involves horizontal and vertical restructuring of programs and services
  (a) within jurisdictions, school districts, and community agencies (e.g., among departments,
     divisions, units, schools, clusters of schools)
  (b) between jurisdictions, school and community agencies, public and private sectors;
     among schools; among community agencies

FIG. 7.1.   Interconnected systems for meeting the needs of all students. From various public domain documents authored by H. S. Adelman and L. Taylor and circulated through the Center for Mental Health in Schools at UCLA. Adapted by permission.

forms of intervention required to appropriately respond to problems and accommodate diversity.

Moreover, given the likelihood that many problems are not discrete, the continuum can be designed to address root causes, thereby minimizing tendencies to develop separate programs for each observed problem. In turn, this enables increased coordination and integration of resources which can increase impact and cost-effectiveness. Ultimately, as indicated in Fig. 7.1, the continuum can be evolved into integrated *systems* by enhancing the way the interventions are connected. Such connections may involve hori-

zontal and vertical restructuring of programs and services (a) within jurisdictions, school districts, and community agencies (e.g., among divisions,
units) and (b) between jurisdictions, school and community agencies, public and private sectors, among clusters of schools, and among a wide range
of community resources.

Integrating with School Reform

It is one thing to stress the desirability of developing a full continuum of interventions; it is quite another to propose that schools should be involved in
doing so. In the long run, the success of such proposals probably depends
on anchoring them in the context of the mission of schools. That is, the recommendations must be rooted in the reality that schools are first and fore-
most accountable for educating the young. In particular, such proposals
must reflect an appreciation that schools tend to become concerned about
addressing a problem when it clearly is a barrier to student *learning*. Moreover, it is the entire constellation of external and internal barriers to learning that argues for schools, families, and communities working together to
develop a cohesive, comprehensive, multifaceted approach. Indeed, to
achieve their educational mission, schools need to address barriers to learning and to do so with more than school-linked, integrated health and human services. Addressing barriers involves comprehensive, multifaceted
strategies that can be achieved only through strong school–community
connections. School–community connections are particularly important in
poverty areas where schools often are the largest piece of public real estate
in the community and also may be the single largest employer.

As stressed earlier, however, the current situation is one where schools
marginalize everything but efforts to improve teaching and enhance the
way schools are managed. Therefore, we suggest that policymakers must
move beyond what fundamentally is a two-component model dominating
school reform.

Though improving instruction and the management of schools obviously are essential, our work points to the need for a three-component
framework for reform (see Adelman, 1996a, 1996b; Adelman & Taylor,
1994, 1997, 1998a; Center for Mental Health in Schools, 1996, 1997, 1998,
2000). The third component is conceived as fundamental and essential for
developing comprehensive, multifaceted approaches to enable learning by
addressing barriers (e.g., thus we call it an enabling component).

When current policy and practice are viewed through the lens of this
third component, it becomes evident how much is missing in prevailing efforts to enable learning, development, and teaching. The third component
provides both a basis for combating marginalization and a focal point for
developing a comprehensive framework for policy and practice. When
such a component is elevated to a high policy level, it finally will be feasible

to unify disparate approaches to preventing and ameliorating psychosocial problems and promoting wellness, thereby reducing fragmentation.

Emergence of a cohesive component to enable learning, of course, requires policy reform and operational restructuring that allow for weaving together what is available at a school, expanding this through integrating school, community, and home resources, and enhancing access to community resources by connecting and linking as many as feasible to programs at the school. We see expanded school reform as a foundation upon which to mesh resources for minimizing risk factors and fostering healthy development. At the same time, there must be a rethinking of community resources and how they can best be connected with schools.

It is important to reiterate that a component to address barriers is central to a school's instructional mission and current activity. In policy and practice, all categorical programs, such as Title I, safe-school and drug-free-school programs, and special education, can be integrated into such a comprehensive component. Of course, accomplishing this requires developing new types of mechanisms that can coordinate and eventually integrate school–community–home resources. This brings us to the topic of infrastructure.

BUILDING AN INTERVENTION INFRASTRUCTURE FROM LOCALITIES OUTWARD

Effective school–home–community partnerships require an infrastructure of organizational and operational mechanisms to provide oversight, leadership, resource development, and ongoing support. They are used to (a) arrive at decisions about resource allocation, (b) maximize systematic and integrated planning, implementation, maintenance, and evaluation of existing activity, (c) reach out to expand formal working relationships, and (d) upgrade and modernize in ways that reflect the best intervention thinking and use of technology. These tasks require that staff at various levels adopt some new roles and functions and that families, youth, and other representatives of the community enhance their involvement. The work also calls for redeployment of existing resources, as well as finding new ones.

From the perspective of decentralization, the necessary infrastructure should not be conceived as a hierarchy that starts centrally and works its way down to localities. Rather, the process should be one of building from localities outward. That is, first the focus is on mechanisms at the school–neighborhood level. Then, based on analyses of what is needed to facilitate and enhance efforts at a locality, mechanisms are conceived that enable several school–neighborhood–home collaborations to work together to increase efficiency and effectiveness and achieve economies of scale. Then, systemwide mechanisms are (re)designed to provide support for what each locality is trying to develop. Such a process is highly supportive of the intent to evolve a comprehensive continuum of interventions that plays out effectively in *every locality*. A few examples may help clarify these points and highlight some emerging ideas.

Site-Based Leadership and a Resource-Oriented Team

No matter how well intentioned and motivated participants may be, creating school–community connections takes careful planning and the development of well-conceived mechanisms that ensure school–community– home partnerships coalesce effectively at the local level and are appropriately sanctioned and endowed by governance bodies. A school and its surrounding community are a reasonable focal point around which to build a multilevel organizational plan. Such a focus meshes nicely with contemporary restructuring views that stress increased school-based and neighborhood control.

First mechanisms include designated leadership at the school and a resource-oriented team (e.g., a Resource Coordinating Team) consisting of school and community partners (Adelman, 1993; Adelman & Taylor, 1998b; Rosenblum, DiCecco, Taylor, & Adelman, 1995). Properly constituted, a resource team steers the development of local partnerships and ensures maintenance and improvement of a multifaceted and integrated continuum of interventions. For example, with respect to substance abuse prevention, such a team can help reduce fragmentation and enhance cost-efficacy by analyzing, planning, coordinating, integrating, monitoring, evaluating, and strengthening ongoing efforts.

A resource-oriented team differs from those created to review students (such as a student assistance or success team, a teacher assistance team, a case management team). That is, its focus is not on specific cases, but on clarifying resources and their best use. Such a team provides what often is a missing mechanism for managing and enhancing systems to coordinate, integrate, and strengthen interventions. For example, the team can take responsibility for (a) identifying and analyzing activity and resources with a view to improving how problems are prevented and ameliorated, (b) ensuring there are effective systems to promote use of prereferral interventions, referral, case management, and quality assurance processes, (c) guaranteeing procedures for effective program management and for communication among school and community staff and with the home, and (d) exploring ways to redeploy and enhance resources—such as clarifying which activities are nonproductive and suggesting better uses for the resources, as well as reaching out to connect with additional resources in the school district, home, and neighborhood.

Creation of resource-oriented teams provides essential mechanisms for starting to weave together existing school, home, and community resources and encourage services and programs to function in an increasingly cohesive way. Such teams also are vehicles for building working relationships and can play a role in solving turf and operational problems, developing plans to ensure availability of a coordinated set of efforts, and generally improving the attention paid to developing comprehensive, integrated approaches for addressing barriers to student learning. Although a resource-oriented team might be created solely around psychosocial programs, such a mechanism is meant to bring together representatives of all major programs and services at a school and in the neighborhood. This includes such school personnel as guidance counselors, safe-school and drug-free-school staff, attendance and dropout counselors, psychologists, nurses, social workers, health educators, special-education personnel, after-school program staff, and bilingual and Title I program coordinators. It also includes representatives of any community agency that is significantly involved with schools and, of course, parents and older students. Beyond these, such a team is well advised to add the energies and expertise of administrators, regular classroom teachers, noncertificated staff, the local business community, the faith community, and others willing to make the commitment.

Where creation of "another team" is seen as a burden, existing teams can be asked to broaden their scope. At school sites, teams such as student assistance teams, teacher assistance teams, site-based management teams, and school crisis teams have extended their functions to encompass resource mapping, analyses, coordination, and enhancement. To do so, however, they must take great care to structure their agenda so that sufficient time is devoted to the additional tasks.

Most schools and agencies do not have an administrator whose job definition includes the leadership role and functions related to the aforementioned activity. Moreover, most principals or agency heads don't have time to add such a role to their job descriptions. Thus, we find it imperative that a school and agency establish policies and restructure jobs to ensure there is a *site administrative lead* whose job encompasses this role and its many functions. In addition, a site *staff lead* can be identified from the cadre of line staff who have interest and expertise with respect to school–community–home partnerships. If a locality has a center facility (e.g., Family or Parent Resource Center or a Health Center), the center's coordinator would be one logical choice for this role. Such leads must sit on the resource team and then represent and advocate the team's recommendations whenever governance and administrative bodies meet—especially at key times when decisions are made regarding programs and operations (e.g., use of space, time, budget, and personnel). Besides facilitating the development of a potent approach for developing school–community–home partnerships, administrative and staff leads carry out key functions in daily implementation, monitoring, and problem solving of such partnerships.

Building Outward

Conceptualization of the necessary local-level infrastructure helps delineate what supportive mechanisms should be developed to enable several school–neighborhood collaborations to work together (Adelman, 1993; Center for Mental Health in Schools, 1999a, 1999b). Such a perspective also provides the necessary foundation for defining what is needed at systemwide levels to support localities.

Neighboring localities have common concerns and may have programmatic activity that can use the same resources. By sharing, they can eliminate redundancy and reduce costs. Some school districts already pull together clusters of schools to combine and integrate personnel and programs. These are sometimes called complexes or families of schools. Some cities and counties have developed local planning groups involving public and private agencies and community representatives. A multilocality *resource council* provides a key infrastructure mechanism for work at this level. Such councils can help ensure cohesive and equitable deployment of resources and also can enhance the pooling of resources to reduce costs. They can be particularly useful for linking schools and community resources and integrating the efforts of high schools and their feeder middle and elementary schools. Multilocality councils are especially attractive to community agencies who often don't have the time or personnel to link with individual schools. To these ends, one to two representatives from each local resource team can be chosen to form a council, meeting at least once a month. Specifically, such a council helps (a) coordinate and integrate programs serving multiple schools and neighborhoods, (b) identify and meet common needs for capacity building including staff development, and (c) create linkages and collaborations among schools and agencies. More generally, it provides a mechanism for leadership, communication, maintenance, quality improvement, and ongoing development of a comprehensive continuum of programs and services. Natural starting points for councils are the sharing of needs assessment, resource mapping, analyses, and recommendations for reform and restructuring. Specific areas of initial focus may be on such matters as community–school violence and substance abuse and developing comprehensive, multifaceted, and integrated prevention programs.

Local and multisite mechanisms are not sufficient. Systemwide policy guidance, leadership, and assistance are required. In establishing comprehensive approaches and partnerships, a systemwide *policy* commitment represents an essential starting point. Then, systemwide mechanisms must be established and must reflect a clear conception of how each supports local activity. Several systemwide mechanisms seem essential for coherent oversight and leadership in developing, maintaining, and enhancing comprehensive approaches involving school–community–home partnerships. One is a *systemwide leader* with responsibility and accountability for the systemwide vision and strategic planning related to (a) developing collaborations to evolve comprehensive approaches and (b) ensuring coordination and integration of activity among localities and systemwide. The leader's functions also encompass evaluation, including determination of equity in program delivery, quality improvement reviews of all mechanisms and procedures, and ascertaining results.

Two other recommended mechanisms at this level are a *system-wide leadership group* and *a resource-coordinating body* (for a school district/community). The former can provide expertise and leadership for the ongoing evolution of an initiative; the latter can provide guidance for operational coordination and integration across the system. The composition for these should have some overlap. The systemwide resource coordinating body should include representatives of multilocality councils and planning bodies. The leadership group should include (a) key administrative and line staff with relevant expertise and vision, (b) staff who can represent the perspectives of the various stakeholders, and (c) others whose expertise (e.g., public health, mental health, social services, recreation, juvenile justice, postsecondary institutions) make them invaluable contributors.

School Boards

Matters related to comprehensive approaches and school–community–home partnerships appear regularly on the agenda of local school boards. The problem is that each item tends to be handled in an ad hoc manner, without sufficient attention to the whole picture. One result is that the administrative structure in the school district is not organized in ways that coalesce its various functions (programs, services) for addressing barriers and promoting healthy development. The piecemeal structure reflects the marginalized status of such functions and both creates and maintains fragmented policies and practices. Analyses suggest that boards of education need a standing committee that deals in depth and consistently with these matters so they are addressed in more cohesive and effective ways that fully reflect how various resources and functions relate to each other (Center for Mental Health in Schools, 1998).

THE CURRICULUM OF AN ENABLING COMPONENT

Adoption by school policymakers of an enabling component affirms the proposition that a comprehensive, multifaceted, integrated continuum of interventions is essential in addressing the needs of youngsters who encounter barriers interfering with academic progress (e.g., Adelman & Taylor, 1994, 1997; Center for Mental Health in Schools, 1999b). (Note: Enabling is defined as "providing with the means or opportunity; making possible, practical, or easy.") The continuum presented in Fig. 7.1 helps guide development of such a cohesive, integrated approach.

Operationalizing the concept of an enabling component requires an additional framework. This framework outlines six areas of enabling activity we refer to as the component's curriculum. This curriculum encompasses programs to (a) enhance classroom-based efforts to enable learning, (b) provide prescribed student and family assistance, (c) respond to and prevent crises, (d) support transitions, (e) increase home involvement in schooling, and (f) reach out to develop greater community involvement and support (see Fig. 7.2). Each of these is displayed in Fig. 7.2 and is described briefly in the following subsections. (For a fuller description, see Adelman, 1996a; Adelman & Taylor, 1998b.)

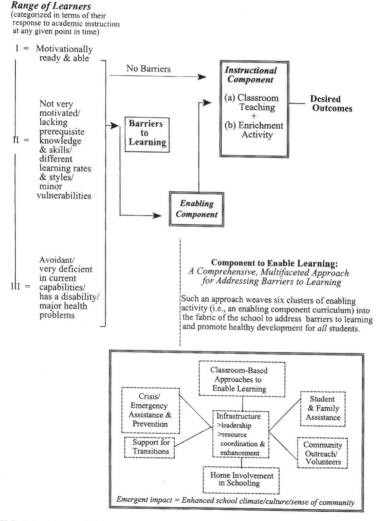

FIG. 7.2. An enabling component to address barriers to learning and enhance healthy development at a school site. (From various public domain documents authored by H. S. Adelman and L. Taylor and circulated through the Center for Mental Health in Schools at UCLA. Adapted by permission.)

Classroom-Focused Enabling.   Programmatic activity to enhance classroom-based efforts to enable learning is accomplished by increasing teachers' effectiveness in accommodating a wider range of individual differences, fostering a caring context for learning, and preventing and handling a wider range of problems when they arise. Such efforts are essential to increasing the effectiveness of classroom instruction, supporting inclusionary policies, and reducing the need for specialized services. Work in this area requires systematic programs to (a) personalize professional development of staff; (b) develop the capabilities of paraeducators, assistants and volunteers, (c) provide temporary out-of-class assistance for students, and (d) enhance resources in the classroom.

Support for Transitions.   Students and their families are regularly confronted with a variety of transitions (e.g., changing schools, changing grades, inclusion from special education, before- and after-school transitions, school-to-work or postsecondary education). Examples of transition programs include (a) schoolwide activities for welcoming new arrivals and ensuring ongoing social supports, (b) articulation strategies to support grade transitions and special-education transitions, (c) before- and after-school and vacation activities to enrich learning and provide recreation in a safe environment, and so forth.

Home Involvement in Schooling.   Among the programs included here are activities to (a) address the learning and support needs of adults in the home, (b) help families learn how to support students with schoolwork, (c) improve communication and connections between home and school, and (d) elicit collaborations and partnerships from those at home to meet school and community needs.

Crisis Assistance and Prevention.   Schools must respond to, minimize the impact of, and prevent crises. This requires systematic programs for (a) emergency response at a school and community wide, and (b) minimizing risk factors to prevent crises related to violence, suicide, child abuse. A key mechanism in this area is development of a crisis team trained in emergency response procedures. The team can take the lead in planning ways to prevent crises by developing programs for conflict mediation and enhancing a caring school culture.

Student and Family Assistance.   This one area encompasses most of the services that are the focus of integrated service models. Social, physical, and mental health assistance available in the school and community are integrated to provide personalized services. Systems for triage, case, and resource management increase consistency and effectiveness.

Community Outreach for Involvement and Support. Most schools do their job better when they are an integral and positive part of the community. For schools to be integral, steps must be taken to create and maintain collaborative connections. Outreach can be made to (a) public and private agencies, (b) higher education, (c) business and professional organizations, (d) churches, and (e) volunteer service organizations. One facet of all this outreach is establishment of programs designed to recruit, train, and maintain volunteers to assist students in school programs.

From a psychological perspective, the impact of developing sound programs related to each area is establishment of an atmosphere that encourages mutual support and caring and creates a sense of community. Such an atmosphere can play a key role in preventing learning, behavior, emotional, and health problems. Caring begins when students and families feel they are truly welcomed at schools and have a range of social supports. School and community programs that promote cooperative learning, peer tutoring, mentoring, human relations, and conflict resolution enhance a caring atmosphere.

The usefulness of the concept of an enabling component as a broad unifying focal point for policy and practice is evidenced in its adoption by various states and localities around the country, such as the California Department of Education (1997) and the Los Angeles Unified School District (1995), whose version is called a *Learning Supports* component, and the Hawaii Department of Education (1999), whose version is called a Comprehensive Student Support System. The concept of an enabling component also has been incorporated into the New American Schools' Urban Learning Center Model (1998) as a break-the-mold school reform initiative. The U.S. Department of Education recognized the Urban Learning Center Model as an important evolving demonstration of comprehensive school reform and has included the design in federal legislation as one of 22 outstanding models that schools are encouraged to adopt. (See Table 7.1 for a description of these pioneering initiatives.)

POLICY SUPPORT FOR SCHOOL–COMMUNITY CONNECTIONS

Ironically, policy simply calling for interagency collaboration to reduce fragmentation and redundancy with a view to greater efficiency may, in the long run, be counterproductive to improving school–community connections. In too many instances, school-linked services result only in colocating community agencies on school campuses. As these activities proceed, a small number of students receive services, but little connection is made with school staff and programs.

Development of a comprehensive, integrated approach that effectively addresses barriers to learning requires cohesive policy that facilitates

TABLE 7.1

A Few Exemplars of Efforts to Restructure Student Supports and Integrate Them With School Reform

New American Schools' Urban Learning Center Model. This is one of the comprehensive school reform designs federal legislation encourages school to adopt. It incorporates a comprehensive, multifaceted, and integrated approach to addressing barriers to learning as a third component of school reform—equal to the instructional and governance components. This third enabling component is called "Learning Supports." In addition to focusing on addressing barriers to learning, there is a strong emphasis on facilitating healthy development, positive behavior, and asset building as the best way to prevent problems. There is a major emphasis on weaving together what is available at a school, expanding these resources through integrating school/community/home resources, and enhancing access to community resources through formal linkages. A key operational infrastructure mechanism is a resource-oriented team that clarifies resources and their best use. The elements of the learning supports component at each school involve: classroom-focused enabling to ensure a potent focus on commonplace behavior, learning, and emotional problems, support for transitions, crisis assistance and prevention, home involvement in schooling, student and family assistance, and community outreach for involvement and support.

Hawaii's Comprehensive Student Support System. This is the umbrella concept under which the state's Department of Education is developing a continuum of programs/services to support a school–academic, social, emotional, and physical environments so that all students learn. The system provides five level of student support: basic support for all students, informal additional support through collaboration, services through school-level and community programs, specialized services from the Department of Education and/or other agencies, and intensive and multiple agency services. The aim is to align programs and services in a responsive manner to create a caring community. Key elements of the program include personalized classroom climate and differentiated classroom practices, prevention/early intervention, family involvement, support for transitions, community outreach and support, and specialized assistance and crisis/emergency support and follow-through. This range of proactive support requires teaming, organization, and accountability. To help achieve all this, a cadre of school-based and complex level Support Service Coordinators are being trained.

Los Angeles Unified School District. Several years ago, the district formulated a Strategic Plan for Restructuring of Student Health & Human Services. The goals were to (a) increase effectiveness, and efficiency in providing learning supports to students and their families, and (b) enhance partnerships with parents, schools, and community-based efforts to improve outcomes for youth. Building on the same body of work that was used in developing the Urban Learning Center model, the plan called for a major restructuring of school-owned pupil services in order to develop a comprehensive, multifaceted, and integrated "Learning Supports" components to address barriers to learning. Key operational infrastructure mechanisms are a school-based resource team and a cluster coordinating council that focuses on clarifying resources and their best use—all of which are concerned with developing the key elements of the learning supports component at each school. To facilitate restructuring, a cadre of change agents called Organization Facilitators was developed. The plan called for these change agents to assist in establishing the infrastructure at each school and for the high school feeder pattern with the aim of enhancing resource use, as well as integrating other resources from the community.

Community Schools. As exemplified by the Children's Aid Society, Community Schools in New York City is a partnership between the Children's Aid Society, the New York City Board of Education, the school district, and community-based partners. The focus is on a model that is designed to help strengthen the educational process for teachers, parents, and students in a seamless way. The approach combines teaching and learning with the delivery of an array of social, health, child, and youth development services that emphasizes community and parental involvement. Current demonstrations provide on-site child and family support services—from health care clinics and counseling to recreation, extended education, early childhood programs, job training, immigration services, parenting programs, and emergency assistance.

Note. For more exemplars, see http:smhp.psych.ucla.edu. Go to Contents, scroll to Policy Leadership Cadre for MH in Schools, click, and then access the document *Mental Health in Schools: Guidelines, Models, Resources & Policy Considerations.*

blending of many resources. In schools, this includes restructuring to combine parallel efforts supported by general funds, compensatory and special-education entitlement, safe-school and drug-free-school grants, and specially funded projects. In communities, the need is for better ways of connecting agency resources to each other and to schools. The end product should be cohesive and potent school–community partnerships. With proper policy support, a comprehensive approach can be woven into the fabric of every school. Neighboring schools can be linked to share limited resources and achieve powerful school–community connections.

Based on our understanding of the state of the art related to the body of literature that has relevance for creating schoolhome–community partnerships, we can extrapolate some guidelines (Adelman & Taylor, in press). Our intent in doing so is to further underscore the type of policy and systemic changes that researchers and practitioners must be prepared to address if they want to significantly reduce the rates of psychosocial problems that permeate school and community. The guidelines are as follows:

- Move existing *governance* toward shared decision making and appropriate degrees of local control and private-sector involvement—a key facet of this is guaranteeing roles and providing incentives, supports, and training for effective involvement of line staff, families, students, and other community members.
- Create *change teams and change agents* to carry out the daily activities of systemic change related to building essential support and redesigning processes to initiate, establish, and maintain changes over time.
- Delineate high-level *leadership assignments* and underwrite essential *leadership/management training* regarding vision for change, how to effect such changes, how to institutionalize the changes, and how to generate ongoing renewal.
- Establish institutionalized *mechanisms to manage and enhance resources* for school–community partnerships and related systems (focusing on analyzing, planning, coordinating, integrating, monitoring, evaluating, and strengthening ongoing efforts).
- Provide adequate funds for *capacity building* related to both accomplishing desired system changes and enhancing intervention quality over time—a key facet of this is a major investment in staff recruitment and development using well-designed and technologically sophisticated strategies for dealing with the problems of frequent turnover and diffusing information updates; another facet is an investment in technical assistance at all levels and for all aspects and stages of the work.
- Use a sophisticated approach to *accountability* that initially emphasizes data that can help develop effective approaches for collaboration in providing interventions and a results-oriented focus on short-term

benchmarks and that evolves into evaluation of long-range indicators of impact. (Here, too, technologically sophisticated and integrated management information systems are essential.).

Such policy would allow personnel to build the continuum of interventions needed to make a significant impact in addressing the learning, health, and general well-being of all students.

CONCLUDING COMMENTS

Collaboratives involving the school, home, and community are sprouting in a dramatic and ad hoc manner throughout the country. They have the potential for improving schools, strengthening neighborhoods, and leading to a marked reduction in young people's problems. Or, such "collaborations" can end up being another reform effort that promised a lot, but did little. Whereas it is relatively simple to make informal linkages, establishing major long-term partnerships is complicated. They require vision, cohesive policy, and basic systemic reforms. The complications are readily seen in efforts to evolve a comprehensive, multifaceted, and integrated continuum of interventions. Such a continuum clearly involves much more than linking a few services, recreation, and enrichment activities to schools. Major processes are required to develop and evolve formal and institutionalized sharing of a wide spectrum of responsibilities and resources. And, the intent must be to sustain such partnerships over time.

Comprehensive school–home–community partnerships represent a promising direction for efforts to generate essential interventions to address barriers to learning, enhance healthy development, and strengthen families and neighborhoods. They broaden resources and strategies to enhance caring contexts that support student success. Such partnerships must weave together a critical mass of resources and strategies to enhance caring communities that support all youth and their families and enable success at school and beyond.

Clearly, getting from here to there involves major challenges. From a local perspective, there are three overlapping challenges in developing partnerships for comprehensive, multifaceted programs. One involves weaving existing school resources together. A second entails evolving programs so they are more effective. For this to happen in optimal ways, there must be an extensive restructuring of all school-owned activity, such as pupil services, safe-school and drug-free-school initiatives, and special- and compensatory-education programs. There also must be full integration of such activity with the instructional and management components. The third challenge is to reach out to additional resources and broaden the range of partnerships (e.g., formally connecting school programs with assets at home and in the business and faith communities, as well as collaborating with enrichment, recreation, and service resources in the neighborhood). It is through creating and maintaining collaborations with home and community that schools will not only enhance their effectiveness, but will also clearly be seen as an integral part of the neighborhoods in which they reside.

And, of course, addressing these challenges requires reframing the roles of professionals who work in schools and communities. Their new roles will entail multifaceted functions—providing vision and leadership that transforms how schools and communities address barriers to learning and enhance health development.

In highlighting the aforementioned matters, we have sketched out new directions for advancing policy and practice (and research). We have also noted that pioneering efforts are under way. It is encouraging that such important systemic changes are in the works.

CHAPTER ACTIVITIES

For Discussion

1. In the chapter, the authors offer the following propositions:

   We suggest that many specific problems are best pursued as an integrated part of a comprehensive, multifaceted continuum of interventions designed to address barriers to learning and promote healthy development. For another, we submit that comprehensive, multifaceted approaches are feasible only if the resources of schools, families, and communities are woven together. A corollary of this is that the committed involvement of school, family, and community is essential in maximizing intervention implementation and effectiveness.

   What do the authors mean by these statements?

2. What national policies and practices operate for/against effective school–community connections? Make two lists, one "for" and one "against." Include a statement explaining each and the reason for its inclusion in one or the other list.

3. Do the same for state policies in your state.

4. Do the same for local policies in your district.

Case Study

Mary began teaching in an urban school in a midwestern city of approximately 200,000 people. She returned to her hometown in a small college town to student teach from a Big Ten university in a small college town because there were not enough student-teaching placements nearer to the university. Not expressing a preference for placement, she was assigned to an inner-city school in a neighborhood that was largely African-American and low in terms of socioeconomic status. During her semester of student teaching, a first-grade teacher resigned for personal reasons and Mary was offered the position contingent upon successful completion of her student-teaching experience.

Mary was White and had been raised by professional parents—her mother was a history teacher and her father a pharmacist—in an upper-middle-class neighborhood. Although beginning to teach in the same town, she soon discovered that her personal experiences and those of her students were widely disparate. She felt as if she were in foreign territory as indeed she was. During her early school years, Mary's parents had made sure that she ate her oatmeal before leaving for school. Her father always gave her loose change to spend at the school snack shop. Her mother took her to the best department stores to buy new outfits each season. For Christmas and birthdays, she was lavished with gifts. Mary had a personal relationship with her dentist due to all of the cavities that resulted from visits to her father's corner drugstore with its candy counter. The family doctor was a personal friend of her parents. During the summer, Mary and her family traveled extensively in the United States and Canada.

Mary's students were having quite different experiences as they grew up, in fact even at 6 and 7 years old, some of them had already lost their childhood. Many in her class lived in government projects constructed during the civil rights movement of the 1960s. Not constructed of the best materials in the first place, after 30 years, they were a nightmare. Boards covered windows where there had been fires. The halls and grounds were littered with trash. Needing paint, both inside and outside walls were dull, chipped, and cracked. Residents on the upper floors experienced roof leaks and residents on lower floors experienced leaks from faulty plumbing.

Many students in her class came to school unfed and dirty. Many were late having had to care for younger siblings before starting out. Getting to school could be harrowing, not only from the standpoint of school-age bullies, but also from drug dealers who hung out on street corners and in alleyways. Having arrived, the students were not necessarily ready and eager to learn. They were often tired, hungry, and not trusting of this young White woman who was their teacher. If they had an ear infection, or needed medication for ADD/ADHD, the chances were slim that there was money for either. The breakfast and lunch programs provided the only meals that some of the students had during the week, but often, ignored dental needs made eating painful.

Parents of her students were certainly not uncaring! Often, several parents would stop by before or after school to ask about their child's progress and how they might help. Many however were nonreaders themselves. Sometimes the parents were not home to help and so the need for the students to care for their brothers and sisters. The parents were not out carousing; rather many were working two jobs to break the welfare cycle. One young mother in particular often asked Mary's advice on childrearing. She was a beautiful woman, slight with olive skin and huge eyes. She and her daughter were always immaculately groomed. She was a single parent with four children younger than Melvina who was in Mary's class. Mary was at a loss as to how to respond. She couldn't imagine being 19 with five children under the age of 6 and trying to raise them alone in this neighborhood!

Mary wondered where to begin! Should she focus on her classroom only and ignore the environment? But the children needed sound nutrition and health care. The parents needed support in their efforts to improve their own current reality and their children's future. How might the school and its neighborhood begin to work together to build a true school–community relationship that would benefit everyone?

   1.   Refer to Fig. 7.2. Think about Mary's students in terms of this diagram. What are the barriers that they face? Which of the following six curricular areas of an enabling component might Mary begin with in her efforts to address the barriers?

   •   Student and family assistance.
   •   Community outreach/volunteers.
   •   Home involvement in schooling.
   •   Support for transitions.
   •   Crisis/emergency assistance and prevention.
   •   Classroom-focused enabling.
Begin a plan for her to pursue.

   2.   Refer to Fig. 7.1. Which level on the continuum should Mary focus on at first? How can she work with others at the school and in the community to develop a comprehensive, multifaceted approach that encompasses each of the following levels?

   •   Systems for prevention.
   •   Systems of early intervention.
   •   Systems of care.

REFERENCES

Adelman, H. S. (1993). School-linked mental health interventions: Toward mechanisms for service, coordination and integration. *Journal of Community Psychology, 21*, 309—319.

Adelman, H. S. (1996a). Restructuring education support services and integrating community resources: Beyond the full service school model. *School Psychology Review, 25,* 431–445.

Adelman, H. S. (1996b). *Restructuring support services: Toward a comprehensive approach.* Kent, OH: American School Health Association.

Adelman, H. S., & Taylor, L. (1993). School-based mental health: Toward a comprehensive approach. *Journal of Mental Health Administration, 20,* 32–45.

Adelman, H. S., & Taylor, L. (1994). *On understanding intervention in psychology and education.* Westport, CT: Praeger.

Adelman, H. S., & Taylor, L. (1997). Addressing barriers to learning: Beyond school-linked services and full service schools. *American Journal of Orthopsychiatry, 67,* 408–421.

Adelman, H. S., & Taylor, L. (1998a). Involving teachers in collaborative efforts to better address barriers to student learning. *Preventing School Failure, 42*(2), 55–60.

Adelman, H. S., & Taylor, L. (1998b). Reframing mental health in schools and expanding school reform. *Educational Psychologist, 33,* 135–152.

Adelman, H. S., & Taylor, L. (2000). Moving prevention from the fringes into the fabric of school improvement. *Journal of Educational and Psychological Consultation, 11,* 7–36.

Adelman, H. S., & Taylor, L. (in press). Creating school and community partnerships for substance abuse prevention programs. *Journal of Primary Prevention.*

Adler, L., & Gardner, S. (Eds.). (1994). *The politics of linking schools and social services.* Washington, DC: Falmer Press.

Burt, M. R. (1998, November). *Reasons to invest in adolescents.* Paper presnted at the Health Futures of Youth II: Pathways to Adolescent Health conferences. Washington, DC: Maternal and Child Health Bureau, U.S. Department of Health and Human Services.

Cahill, M. (1998, November). *Development of a core set of principles for community strategies to enhance youth health and development.* Paper presented at the Health Futures of Youth II, Pathways to Adolescent Health conferences. Washington, DC: Maternal and Child Health Bureau, U.S. Department of Health and Human Services.

California Department of Education. (1997). *Guide and criteria for program quality review: Elementary.* Sacramento, CA: Author.

Catalano, R. F., & Hawkins, J. D. (1995). Risk-focused prevention—Using the social development strategy. Seattle, WA: Developmental Research and Programs, Inc.

Center for Mental Health in Schools. (1996). *Addressing barriers to learning: Current status and new directions.* Los Angeles: Author.

Center for Mental Health in Schools. (1997). *Addressing barriers to learning: Closing gaps in school–community policy and practice.* Los Angeles: Author.

Center for Mental Health in Schools. (1998). *Restructuring boards of education to enhance schools' effectiveness in addressing barriers to student learning.* Los Angeles: Author.

Center for Mental Health in Schools. (1999a). *Policymakers' guide to restructuring student support resources to address barriers to learning.* Los Angeles: Author.

Center for Mental Health in Schools. (1999b). *School–community partnerships: A guide.* Los Angeles: Author.

Center for Mental Health in Schools. (2000). *Pioneer initiatives to reform education support programs.* Los Angeles: Author.

Dryfoos, J. G. (1994). *Full-service schools: A revolution in health and social services for children, youth and families.* San Francisco: Jossey-Bass.

Dryfoos, J. G. (l998). *Safe passage: Making it through adolescence in a risky society.* New York: Oxford University Press.

Franklin, C., & Streeter, C. L. (1995). School reform: Linking public schools with human services. *Social Work, 40,* 773–782.

Hardiman, P. M., Curcio, J. L., & Fortune, J. C. (1998). School-linked services. *The American School Board Journal, 185,* 37–40.

Hawaii Department of Education. (1999). *Comprehensive student support system guidelines.* Oahu, HA: Author.

Hodgkinson, H. L. (1989). *The same client: The demographics of education and service delivery systems.* Washington, DC: Institute for Educational Leadership, Center for Demographic Policy.

Larner, M. B., Zippiroli, L., & Behrman, R. E. (1999). When school is out: Analysis and recommendations. *The Future of Children, 9,* 4–20.

Los Angeles Unified School District (1995). *Plan for restructuring student health and human services.* Los Angeles: Author.

Melaville, A., & Blank, M. J. (1998). *Learning together: The developing field of school–community initiatives.* Flint, MI: Mott Foundation.

Rosenblum, L., DiCecco, M. B., Taylor, L., & Adelman, H. S. (1995). Upgrading school support programs through collaboration: Resource coordinating teams. *Social Work in Education, 17,* 117–24.

Schorr, L. B. (1997). *Common purpose: Strengthening families and neighborhoods to rebuild America.* New York: Anchor Books.

Urban Learning Center Model. (1998). *A design for a new learning community.* Los Angeles: CA: Los Angeles Educational Partnership.

8

Peaceable School Communities: Morality and the Ethic of Care

Linda P. Thurston
Kansas State University

Terry R. Berkeley
Towson University

> To educate a person in mind but not in morals is a menace to society.
> —T. Roosevelt

> A question ain't really a question if you know the answer too.
> —J. Prine

> The best thing for disturbances of the spirit ... is to learn.
> —T. H. White

Recently on National Public Radio's "Morning Edition" it was reported that "In Butte, MT, the Superintendent of Schools now has principals in the district hold regular safety drills for their students, teachers, assistants, and other staff in light of the recent spate of publicized attacks of violence taking place in American schools, especially those taking place in rural schools."

In the past, thoughts of a little red schoolhouse evoke feelings of warmth and security, of coziness and caring. In small communities, for example, the schoolhouse brings visions of friendly neighbors, barn-raisings, Fourth of July picnics, and people standing in the middle of the street exchanging news, where everybody drives a pickup truck and you wave at folks, whether you know them or not. Part of this picture, both stereotype and reality, impact schools and the ability of educators to provide safe, caring learning environments for students.

The Berenstain Bears, truck and jeans advertisements, popular movies such as *Hope Floats*, and Dolly Parton songs promote an idealized image of "community" that is as unrealistic as it is rarefied. In some cases, America is seen as a place of green grass, white fences, clean water, and simple living. This image is crime free, problem free, and carefree. Black leather and low-riders are just passing through on their way to Sturgis.

Other stereotypes may be rooted in tradition and history. When university students were asked about their perceptions of "rural," their attitudes about characteristics included the importance of a sense of community and of peace, safety, and relationship (Herzog & Pittman, 1995). Other stereotypic characteristics included slow pace, quietness, and an ethic of helping others with residents seen as independent, honest, simple, and religious. Stereotypes and other generalizations do injustice to the real lives of American families and communities, whether rural or urban.

These are ecological, occupational, and sociological aspects of a community. Though a rural community may be more homogeneous than an urban community, communities are different from each other (Ayalon, 1995). In rural areas and in urban, there is great diversity with differences starting "at the beginning of the Appalachian Trail in Maine and through portions of the South, the Midwest, the West, and Native American fishing communities, ... in the Northwest" (Berkeley & Bull, 1995, p. 11).

In rural areas, it sometimes seems easier to recognize the interdependence of children, their families, schools, and communities. Schools often are the focal point of the community and serve as a source of community integration, a source of pride, social cohesion, and local identification (Ayalon, 1995). But these same characteristics could easily apply to schools in the barrios of San Antonio and other urban schools. A sense of community and smallness of scale (Herzog & Pittman, 1995), and a sense of oneness among community members and community connectedness (Smithmier, 1994) represent qualities of rural life. Thus, cooperation and participation are traditional concepts. Rural cooperatives are common and have been the keystone to economic viability (Smithmier, 1994). Cooperatives have extended beyond the economic sector to become an essential means of providing special education and related services to students in remote rural areas that do not have ready access to resources as do urban school districts. Interdependence, community connectedness, and cooperation are commonalities inherent in rural communities and schools.

VIOLENCE AND CONFLICT

Some students do not seem to feel safe in school (Reed & Strahan, 1995; Srebalus, Schwartz, Vaughan, & Tunick, 1996) with school safety being a concern of school board members (Wanat, 1996) and parents (Thurston & Navarrete, 1996). It is a concern for which administrators (Ballard & Mc-Coy, 1996) and counselors (Caldarella, Sharpnack, Loosli, & Merrell, 1996; Srebalus, et al., 1996) do not feel prepared to manage or resolve.

Although there is less crime in rural areas than in their urban counterparts, rural areas now have more crime and violence than they have in the past and some problems are serious (Bachus, 1994; Donnermeyer, 1994). Violence in schools was worse in 1998 than in the 5 years previous according to Peterson, Beekley, Speaker, and Pietrzak (1998). In their survey, 22% of rural respondents reported an increase in violence at the preschool level, 40% at the elementary school level, 52% at the middle school level, and 43% saw an increase in violence at the high school level.

There are other effects. Violence in schools and communities undermines children's health, mental health, readiness to learn, and ability to learn. School violence also increases the cost of education and makes teacher recruitment and retention difficult (Ballard & McCoy, 1996).

Violence in schools has causes that originate elsewhere. It is a community problem calling for community-based solutions. According to Brendtro and Long (1995), chronic violence is a sign that something may be awry in the community. Caldarella et al. (1996) found that often children who were referred for special education or remedial services had been victims of violence or had witnessed violence. Peterson et al. (1998) found that victims and perpetrators of violence were students who were having academic problems. A dilemma is that some students believe they have no alternative to victimizing others (Dill & Haberman, 1995). Changes in traditional culture and the new demographics in rural as well as urban communities have brought violence and conflict to the fore in those locales. For example, in reviews of research on rural culture, rural areas often are found to be socially conservative, prejudicial, ethnocentric, and intolerant to nonconforming ideas (Ayalon, 1995). It is in rural communities that White supremacy groups were born and hate groups established bases of operations (Donnermeyer, 1994). In turn, prejudice and intolerance can pose significant problems for school safety, school climate, and inclusive education.

Educational, economic, and demographic trends pose challenges for citizens in all communities and educators in schools. These trends include increasing cultural and economic diversity, aging, depopulation, and rapid changes in communication and other technology (Ward, 1994). Schools and communities often are doubly affected by these changes because they are tied together in a way that most urban and suburban schools are not. Hobbs (1994) suggested that in small communities there is increasing personal and family stress, weakened social and economic ties of residents to their communities, loss of social and economic functions of schools, government, and health care as they cease to be locally controlled. He pointed to a diminished sense of community and growing sense of powerlessness as outside forces affect life with resources often being beyond their sphere of control.

PREVENTION AND INTERVENTION: THE ETHIC OF CARE

Attitudes and popular images about the meaning and nature of rural life mask several important issues related to preventing violence and conflict in schools. Harrington-Lueker (1993) believed the biggest obstacle in fighting bias and intolerance leading to violence and conflict is the widespread sense of denial that it exists. Rural residents often assume drugs, crime, poverty, and suicide are concerns for urban America (Bachus, 1994; Dorrell, 1993; Peterson, et al., 1998). Because of ideological attitudes and stereotypes, citizens and school personnel may not see problems of conflict and violence in their communities. In rural communities, more so than in urban or suburban areas, informal social relationships are relatively more important in influencing individual behavior, thus masking recognition of all sorts of problems and tensions (Blaser, 1994; Donnermeyer, 1994).

Schools and communities can establish a foundation for preventing and reducing violence and many of its underlying causes. Positive school climate is a key to reducing and preventing violence and other similar concerns. Many schools strive to create safe, inclusive environments for all students. Wanat (1996) described a safe school as one in which students and teachers feel free of physical, psychological, and emotional abuse.

We like the term *peaceable school* instead of *safe school*. Our belief is that peace is the state in which each individual exercises his or her responsibilities to ensure that all individuals can enjoy all of the rights accorded to them and in which every individual is able to survive and thrive without being hampered by conflict, prejudice, hatred, antagonism, or injustice (Bodine, Crawford, & Schrumpf, 1994). The pervasive theme in a peaceable school is for all human interactions to be based on an ideal of valuing human dignity and esteem. For us, it is a warm and caring community characterized by cooperation, communication, tolerance, positive emotional expression, and conflict resolution (Kreidler, 1984).

Although many schools have success with metal detectors, communications technology (Ballard & McCoy, 1996; Watson, 1995), and exclusionary policies such as Zero Tolerance (Litke, 1996), the focus we believe in is curricular and interactive because it is based on the theme of care and the valuing of human dignity. These suggestions fit the caring model and focus on preventing violence as well as developing and nurturing global values associated with morality and justice. These are proactive strategies for promoting peaceable schools equally applicable in urban settings.

STRATEGIES TO CARING

Today's communities and families are facing a changing world of complex and confusing values. The rebirth of interest in character education, moral education, and the ethic of care, in part, is due to the violence and conflict in schools and society. Children need assistance in learning to make moral decisions based on the values of respect and responsibility (Tyree, Vance, & McJunkin, 1997). Educators need to address these values through a caring curriculum and school environment, whether they teach on the Alaskan tundra or the streets of Brooklyn. Power and Makogon (1996) suggested that caring flows out of interpersonal connections and involves a sensitive responsiveness to others' experiences as well as feelings of concern and solicitude of others. Lickona (1993) called for making respect and responsibility the fourth and fifth R's in our schools.

The ethic of care is essential to effective teaching. Noddings (1995), the leading theorist and proponent regarding themes of caring in educational settings, suggested caring should be part of the cultural literacy schools and communities impart, and themes of care should take education beyond systematic and sequential learning of content. In addition, she believed we will not attain success in academic achievement until children believe that they themselves are cared for and learn to care for others. According to Noddings and others, developing students with a strong capacity to care is a major objective of responsible education.

Chaskin and Rauner (1995) discussed caring as "an umbrella concept encompassing and connecting a range of discrete characteristics including as empathy, altruism, pro social behavior and efficacy" (p. 670). Caring is a value grounded in relationships informing and guiding people, programs, and institutions. Caring in schools is vital for developing, caring, respectful, and responsible students. Caring creates an atmosphere conducive to learning. In summarizing a thematic issue of Phi Delta Kappan, Lipsitz (1995) suggested human beings need caring in order to thrive without conflict. Communities, she asserted, become violent battlegrounds without the concept of caring.

CATEGORIES OF CARING IN SCHOOLS

There are different ways to attain the goal of peaceable schools and caring communities. The culture of schooling can be subtly and systematically shifted to allow for the development of caring relationships and to foster the values of respect, empathy, human kindness, and justice. Caring can be inculcated into schools as an identifiable factor in students' environments and their relationships with others. This was done in Kohlberg's *Just Community Program* (located in Cambridge, MA, and other places) via the design and implementation of various curricular activities (e.g., social skills, mediation, and conflict resolution training), and through the development of interactional models (e.g., the hidden curriculum of everyday school and classroom life).

Models for Prevention of Violence and Conflict

Noddings (1995) called for a reorganization of the school curriculum and environments around the themes of care. Kist-Kline and Quantz (1998) described a school in which there is an embracing of institutional caring involving political, social, and educational policies and practices. Attanucci (1996) discussed a similar program in which a small high school was organized into smaller groups of 15 to 20 students. Rossi, Vergun, and Weise (1997) described an alternative program based on a strong sense of community with its small numbers of students.

The Just Community rests on Kohlberg's theory of moral reasoning. Students are linked together as a caring moral community (Tyree et al., 1997). In this approach, the building of a community is an explicit and intrinsic goal. According to Power and Makogon (1996), this is a prerequisite for building community in schools of small size. Cohesiveness, teamwork, and group morale are stressed throughout each school day. Students learn justice and care through the practice and experience of justice and caring with responsibility for assuring justice and caring are established and persist. Such small, cohesive, family-like school communities recognize the individuality of each child providing a much needed continuity of context for learning and caring as students move through grades.

Curricular Models for Prevention of Violence and Conflict

Classroom management, curricular focus, and instructional method can embody ongoing moral lessons about how to treat other people, how to treat oneself, and how to regard the process of education (Hansen, 1996). Curriculum needs to be selected or developed with caring in mind. Ryan (1996) specified this be done with collaborative multidisciplinary teams focusing on heroes and heroines, the study of virtues that contribute to a fully human life, learning to reason, and opportunities to be of service to one another and to those in the community.

In his study of multicultural education in America, Ayalon (1995) found that learning and appreciating one's own background is a prerequisite for understanding and appreciating others. He suggested that all students learn about their communities. Specific curricular practices recommended include training for increasing social competency, problem solving, and alternatives to violence. These approaches also include social-skills training (Johnson & Johnson, 1995; Peterson et al., 1998), conflict resolution (Johnson & Johnson, 1995; Lickonia, 1993; Reed & Strahan, 1995), and the use of cooperative learning (Johnson & Johnson, 1995; Lickona, 1993; Lindmark, Marshall, Riley, &

Strey, 1996; Tebben, 1995). Additionally, Curwin (1995) noted the inclusion of the following curricular elements for effective antiviolence campaigns in schools: teaching students alternatives to violence, teaching students how to make more effective decisions, and modeling for students alternative expressions of anger, frustration, and impatience.

Interactional Models for Prevention of Violence and Conflict

Everyday classroom life, including rituals, connections, and interactions, conveys either respect or disrespect for students and for learning. Students in caring learning environments believe the teacher likes and trusts them. Lickona (1993) discussed a holistic approach in considering and involving the school environment as well as the affective aspects of teachers who serve as role models and mentors who strive to develop a cohesive caring classroom community. Learning beyond the formal curriculum takes place and the personal manifestations of care by school personnel are more important in children's lives than any particular curriculum or pattern of pedagogy (Noddings, 1995).

Bulach, Brown, and Potter (1998) noted categories of behaviors administrators and teachers can use to create a caring learning community: willingness to listen, ability to reduce anxiety, rewarding of appropriate behavior, being a friend, and the appropriate use of positive and negative criticism. Reed and Strahan (1995) suggested a gentle stance toward discipline whereby teachers and administrators focus on individual responses between themselves and students, addressing animosity with dignity and treating challenging students with respect. The key elements are respect, optimism, and trust. Deiro (1997) talked about nurturing strategies at the secondary level that include using appropriate self-disclosure, having high expectations of students, using rituals and traditions in the classroom, and networking with parents and family members.

In his 3-year study of 400 classrooms, Hansen (1996) was convinced that daily classroom life is saturated with moral messages. These messages have as important an impact on students as does the formal curriculum. Caring teachers, he observed, signal through their everyday actions that they esteem good teaching and learning. They demonstrate seriousness of purpose, respect for time and place, respect for one another, and a strong sense of caring about students and connections in the classroom.

Lickona (1993) reported that school staff must help children to understand strong, positive core values and to act upon them in their own lives. Teachers do this, he said, by encouraging moral reflection, fostering caring beyond the classroom, recruiting parents as partners, creating a democratic classroom environment, and developing students' appreciation for learning and their commitment to excellence.

CONCLUSIONS

There is significant concern in American schools about violence and safety. The National Public Radio story mentioned previously as well as other stories in newspapers and on television, the recent proliferation of articles in academic journals and books, and public policy mandates in special education and other areas of elementary and secondary education about discipline are clear indicators of the need to find viable solutions to reduce and eradicate violence in this nation's schools.

In rural America, there is pride in being a model for schools in urban and suburban locales. Historically, the rural school reliance on the strong relationship with the community has been the foundation for many of the best practices that have been implemented over the years in all American schools (Butterworth, 1926; DeYoung, 1991; Helge, 1984; Howley & Eckman, 1997; Nachtigal, 1982; Shen, 1997a, 1997b; Theobald & Nachtigal, 1995).

Now, there is a questioning in America as to the approaches necessary to resolve the dilemmas posed by the most violent acts as well as daily infringements on personal safety in order to assure liberty so all students are able to learn. This is taking place at a time when there is greater diversity and difference than ever before in American schools, both urban and rural.

We have discussed the extent of school violence and the importance of school safety, and note, how the great diversity of America makes it impossible to arrive at a single solution to the issues of violence and similar concern affecting all areas and all levels of education. Recent violence in American schools has included the rural areas of this nation (e.g., Arkansas, Tennessee, Wisconsin, Montana). In response, we have provided some examples of alternatives that could be adopted in any school to address violence and to reaffirm individual and collective safety.

The common link from a rural school perspective is a reiteration of the themes of interdependence, community connections, and a spirit of cooperation. From this foundation, the actions of school personnel, whether urban or rural, should embody, affirm, and model a broad framework that says, "This curriculum, this way of teaching, this way of conducting ourselves, and this way of treating others is based on dignity and respect for all whether internal or external to the school." It is interesting to note that there are benchmarks for implementation, including a proactive, multifaceted approach (Litke, 1996), recognition that no one program works for all (Harrington-Lueker, 1998), and a variety of strategies be used (Ballard & McCoy, 1996). In one instance, these strategies have emerged from a rural state, Vermont, in which the following is envisioned (Vermont Restructuring Collaborative, 1994):

> Imagine a time, when every single child grows to be a competent, caring, productive, responsible individual and citizen. Every child experiences school as a place of challenge, hard work, and engagement in things that matter.

The focus in our schools is on the student—the learner—and not on the school itself. The emphasis is on learning instead of teaching, although teaching is more important than ever.

Children learn at their own pace; what they need to learn and grow drives the school. School failure, once thought all but unavoidable for some, is extremely rare. The children know that in every school at least one adult is watching out for them. (p. 23)

There is another central theme in the peaceable school in the caring community: one does not wait until there is a problem. Those responsible include the teacher, the teaching assistant, administrators, other professionals, support staff, parents, community members, and students. As a Kansas farmer once said, "It doesn't matter who started the problem, all that matters is who is going to fix it!"

One could stop here with that bit of common sense. Yet, there is another set of thoughts we would like to offer about caring. Caring is a habit. The capacity to care and, thus, to be peaceable requires change in attitudes and practice in schools. This is not to say that those who work in schools do not care or are not peaceable. Rather, we believe there is the need to develop what Noddings called a paradigm of caring or what we suggest in developing a language of consistency about caring and attempts at moving toward this kind of peace.

Webb, Shumway, and Shute (1996) posited that the most effective change is implemented by the use of "thoughtful leadership" (p. 51), the opposite of what they called the present state of affairs or "mindless leadership" (p. 51), or that which typically exists in school. Thoughtful leadership, they contended, is manifest when "personal integrity is as important as we have represented it to be to students in this curriculum; therefore, it behooves me to make sure that I am honorable in my work with faculty, staff, and students—that I act congruently with my deepest personal beliefs" (p. 52).

Thoughtful leadership, developed by habit, can be coupled with an adherence to a Children's Bill of Rights. Just as Noddings and others were beginning their first work on caring, Wooden (1976) saw a need to protect children from harm by adults, by other children, and from themselves. In this symbol of caring he suggested the following as rights:

1) All Children have the Right to Freedom so they can enjoy the blessings of liberty;

2) All Children have the Right to a Family and a Home so they can enjoy the protection of those who care for them at all times. In instances when this is not possible, there should be possibilities for there to be constants in the lives of children and children know they are the first priority of those new advocates;

3) All Children have the Right to an Education so that regardless of station in life they can enjoy the development of those talents they possess; and,

4) All Children have the Right to Protection by Laws to they will hot be abused, neglected, harmed, or exploited. (pp. 246–248)

These rights, if they are to be enjoyed, are inextricably linked to the idea of community (in and of itself) as well as to life in the community. Because schools are one of the two or three most important institutions in a community, the interest to care for children goes beyond being just a school concern. This Children's Bill of Rights is an ideal, just as is the notion of peaceable schools and caring communities, thus, we end with the idea that if one cannot work toward an ideal in their work with children, why work at all? This really is about doing good and doing good well.

CHAPTER ACTIVITIES

For Further Discussion

1.   When you think about the rural context, what images come to mind to describe and analyze rural life? What about the urban context—descriptive urban images, analysis of urban life?

2.   In rural places, the notion of community is a popular and important theme. How do rural schools fit into the character of rural communities? How has this relationship changes with the gradual infringement of urban influence into rural areas?

3.   How is caring inferred in descriptions of "community" in rural areas: What causes infusion of caring into rural community? Are the concepts of "caring" and "community" integral to rural institutions such as governmental agencies and local organizations?

4.   If caring is characteristic of rural communities, who is responsible for sustaining it? How are the children taught about caring? How does daily civility relate to caring and how is it modeled for children?

5.   How are the concepts of rural "community" and "caring" demonstrated in the school context?

Case Study

Chalk Buttes Elementary.   Chalk Buttes is a rural school approximately 20 miles southwest of Ekalaka. It is a one-room school building on the great western prairie. The teacher at Chalk Buttes earns approximately $18,000 per year, a high salary for a rural school teacher. To supplement the salary, the school board provides a teacherage, an apartment in the rear third of the school building. A woodburner heats the building. Loggers who work the Custer National Forest provide firewood. Belle Fouche, South Dakota, is the nearest "large town," approximately 75 miles to the south. Travel to Belle Fouche is best in good weather, because the school is off-the-oil. The roads are gravel and are fine when they are dry, but slick, muddy, and rutted when they are wet. During the winter, they may be temporarily closed due to drifting snow. The school has access to the world through a satellite dish affording cable TV and the Internet.

The Chalk Buttes students include the following:

- Two Native Americans—a girl, Rosie, and her brother, Andy Shows-no-fear. Rosie is in kindergarten. Andy is a third grader.
- Two Mexican-American children whose primary language is Spanish. Jay (Jesus) is a second grader and his brother Jorge is in third. Their father came north as a migrant worker and got a permanent job with the loggers.
- One boy, Chris, is in the fifth grade. He has ADHD and takes medication.
- One boy, Josh, aged 10, in the fourth grade, has autism. He has motor problems, communication difficulties, and is socially inept. He seems to be bright, but the autism is pretty severe and interferes with his social interactions and academic achievement.
- One girl, Carrie, in seventh grade, has Down syndrome. She can read at the second-grade level, and is physically mature and tall for her age, making her look older than her 12 years.
- One girl, Janine, is in eighth grade. She will go to Ekalaka for high school next year. She is a good student, scoring at the 99th percentile on standardized achievement tests.

Broncs Central High School. Contrast Chalk Buttes Elementary to Broncs Central High School. Broncs Central, located in a small city of 100,000 residents, is the largest of four high schools in town. Teacher salaries in the city average $32,000 per year. Enrollment reached over 2,400 students this year. Because it is in the central city, Broncs students come from a variety of ethnic and socioeconomic backgrounds. Diversity is expected, recognized, and appreciated by school administrators, faculty, and students, but not always by parents or the community. In fact, neighbors with homes across the street from the school regularly complain about the "smokers" who congregate in their "gothic" attire on the school curb to have a smoke before entering the drug/weapon-free school campus and when they leave at the end of the school day.

Broncs Central faculty is an aging group. Many are eligible for retirement within the next 5 years. It is an interesting phenomenon that even with their limited continuing role in the school, they are not particularly open to mentoring student teachers from a nearby regional university. Generally, the faculty are engaged, professionally adept in their individual fields, often recipients of local, state, and national teaching awards, and active in the local professional education association. Several are working on portfolios toward National Board for Professional Teaching Standards certification. They tend to be insular in their interactions with each other, keeping to their own departments and maintaining long-standing friendships with faculty in the same discipline.

To Do

1. Make lists comparing and contrasting these two school environments. How would you expect the concept of "community" to be similar or different in the two?

2. Are there multicultural aspects of "caring"? How do you know? How might these manifest themselves in the two environments as described?

3. To evaluate extent of caring in a community, the following set of variables can be used:

- People and their roles in the community.
- Responsibilities or functions in the community.
- Outcomes or actions/associations (based on roles and responsibilities).

How would you evaluate caring in Chalk Buttes and at Broncs Central based on the aforementioned variables? Are there other variables you might consider in the evaluation of caring?

4. Common themes in rural literature include:

- Interdependence.
- Community connections.
- Spirit of cooperation.

How might these themes exhibit themselves at Chalk Buttes Elementary and/or Broncs Central? How might Broncs Central be reorganized into the ideal of a rural caring community?

REFERENCES

Attanucci, J. S. (1996). Placing care in the human life cycle. *Journal for a Just and Caring Education, 2*(1), 25–41.

Ayalon, A. (1995). Does multicultural education belong in rural white America? *Rural Educator 16*(3), 1–6 & 31.

Bachus, G. (1994). Violence is no stranger in rural schools. *The School Administrator, 51*(4), 18–22.

Ballard, C., & McCoy, D. (1996). Preventing violence in rural schools: A sampling of the responses of school superintendents in southern Georgia. *Small Town, 27*(1), 12–17.

Blaser, J. (1994). Violence and substance abuse in rural America. In J. Blaser (Ed.), *Perspectives on violence and substance use in rural America* (pp. 1–4). Chicago: North Central Regional Educational Laboratory.

Berkeley, T. R., & Bull, K. S. (1995). Voices in rural special education: Retrospectives, prospectives, possibilities. *Rural Special Education Quarterly, 14*(2), 10–16.

Bodine, R. J., Crawford, D. K., & Schrumpf, F. (1994). *Creating the peaceable school.* Champaign, IL: Research Press.

Brendtro, L., & Long, N. (1995). Breaking the cycle of conflict. *Educational Leadership, 52*(5), 52–56.

Bulach, C., Brown, C., & Potter, L. (1998). Behaviors that create a caring learning community. *Journal for a Just and Caring Education, 4*(4), 441–453.

Butterworth, J. E. (1926). *Rural school administration.* New York, NY: Macmillan.

Caldarella, P., Sharpnack, J., Loosli, T., & Merrell, K. W. (1996). The spread of youth gangs into rural areas: A survey of school counselors. *Rural Special Education Quarterly, 15*(4), 18–27.

Chaskin, R. J., & Rauner, D. M. (1995). Youth and caring: An introduction. *Phi Delta Kappan, 76,* 667–674.

Curwin, R. L. (1995). A humane approach to reducing violence in schools. *Educational Leadership, 52*(5), 72–75.

Deiro, J. (1997). Teacher strategies for nurturing healthy connections with students. *Journal for a Just and Caring Education, 3*(2), 192–202.

DeYoung, A. J. (Ed.). (1991). *Rural education: Issues and practices.* New York: Garland Press.

Dill, V. S., & Haberman, M. (1995). Building a gentler school. *Educational Leadership, 52*(5), 69–71.

Donnermeyer, J .F. (1994). Crime and violence in rural communities. In J. Balser (Ed.), *Perspectives on violence and substance use in rural America* (pp. 27–64). Chicago: North Central Regional Educational Laboratory.

Dorrell, L. D. (1993). *You can't look forward to tomorrow, while holding onto yesterday: Rural education and the at-risk student* (Report No. RC 019 500). Burlington, VT: Project Head Start. (ERIC Document Reproduction Service No. ED 367 518)

Hansen, D. T. (1996). Teaching and the moral life of classrooms. *Journal for a Just and Caring Education, 2*(1), 59–74.

Harrington-Lueker, D. (1993). Teaching tolerance. *The Executive Educator, 15*(5), 14–19.

Helge, D. (1984). The state of the art of rural special education. *Exceptional Children, 50*(4), 294–305.

Herzog, M. J. R., & Pittman, R. B. (1995). Home, family, and community: Ingredients in the rural education equation. *Phi Delta Kappan, 77*(2), 113–118.

Hobbs, D. (1994). The context of rising rates of rural violence and substance abuse: The problems and potential of rural communities. In J. Balser (Ed.), *Perspectives on violence and substance use in rural America* (pp. 115–126). Chicago North Central Regional Educational Laboratory.

Howley, C., & Eckman, J. (1997). *Sustainable small schools.* Charleston, WV: ERIC Clearinghouse on Rural Education and Small Schools.

Johnson, D. W., & Johnson, R. T. (1995). Why violence prevention programs don't work—and what does. *Educational Leadership, 52*(5), 63–68.

Kist-Kline, G. E., & Quantz, R. A. (1998). Understanding a school-based mental health program. *Journal for a Just and Caring Education, 4*(3), 307–322.

Kreidler, W. J. (1984). *Creative conflict resolution: More than 200 activities for keeping peace in the classroom—K–6.* Glenview, IL: Scott, Foresman.

Lickona, T. (1993). The return of character education. *Educational Leadership, 50,* 6–11.

Lindmark, T. C., Marshall, J., Riley, S., & Strey, E. (1996). *Improving behavior and academic success through a caring classroom* (Report No. CG 027 343). Rockford, IL: Saint Xavier University & IRI/Skylight Field-Based Master's Program. (ERIC Document Reproduction Service No. ED 399 493)

Lipsitz, J. (1995). Prologue: Why we should care about caring. *Phi Delta Kappan, 76*(9), 665–666.

Litke, C. D. (1996). When violence came to our rural school. *Educational Leadership International, 54*(1), 77–80.

Nachtigal, P. M. (Ed.). (1982). *Rural education: In search of a better way.* Boulder, CO: Westview Press.

Noddings, N. (1995). Teaching themes of caring. *Phi Delta Kappan, 76,* 675–679.

Peterson, G. J., Beekley, C. Z., Speaker, K. M., & Pietrzak, D. (1998). An examination of violence in three rural school districts. *Rural Educator, 19*(3), 25–32.

Power, F. C., & Makogon, T. A. (1996). The just-community approach to care. *Journal for a Just and Caring Education, 2*(1), 9–24.

Reed, C., & Strahan, D. B. (1995). Gentle discipline in violent times. *Journal for a Just and Caring Education, 1,* 320–334.

Rossi, R. J., Vergun, P. B., & Weise, L. J. (1997). Serving rural youth at risk: A portrait of collaboration and community. *Journal of Education for Students Placed at Risk, 2,* 213–227.

Ryan, K. (1996). Character education in the United States: A status report. *Journal for a Just and Caring Education, 2*(1), 75–84.

Shen, J. P. (Ed.). (1977a). *Education in rural America: A reassessment of conventional wisdom.* Boulder, CO: Westview Press.

Shen, J. P. (1997b). The evolution of violence in schools. *Educational Leadership, 55*(2), 18–20.

Smithmier, A. (1994). Constructing a culture of community: The contributions of rural youth. *Journal of Research in Rural Education, 10,* 89–96.

Srebalus, D. J., Schwartz, J. L., Vaughan, R. V., & Tunick, R. H. (1996). Youth violence in rural schools: Counselor perceptions and treatment resources. *The School Counselor, 44,* 48–54.

Tebben, S. L. (1995). Community and caring in a college classroom. *Journal for a Just and Caring Education, 1,* 335–344.

Theobald, P., & Nachtigal, P. (1995). Culture, community, and the promise of education. *Phi Delta Kappan, 77*(2), 132–135.

Thurston, L. P., & Navarrete, L. (1996). A tough row to hoe: Research on education and rural poor families. In *Proceedings of American Council on Rural Special Education (ACRES)* Baltimore: American Council on Rural Special Education.

Tyree, C., Vance, M., & McJunkin, M. (1997). Teaching values to promote a more caring world: A moral dilemma for the 21st century. *Journal for a Just and Caring Education, 3*(2), 215–226.

Vermont Restructuring Collaborative. (1994). *Field guide to educational renewal.* Brandon, VT: Holistic Education Press.

Wanat, D. L. (1996). Defining safe schools: A prerequisite for policy development. *Journal for a Just and Caring Education, 2,* 121–132.

Ward, J. G. (1994). *Looking at rural schools and communities in the 21st century: The impact of changing demographics and economics* (Report No. RC 020 798). Champaign-Urbana, IL: Rural School Development Outreach Project. (ERIC Document Reproduction Service No. ED 401 074)

Watson, R. (1995). A guide to violence prevention. *Educational Leadership, 52*(5), 57–59.

Webb, C. D., Shumway, L. K., & Shute, R. W. (1996). *Local schools of thought: A search for purpose in rural education.* Charleston, WV: ERIC Clearinghouse on Rural Education and Small Schools.

Wooden, K. (1976). *Weeping in the playtime of others: America's incarcerated children.* New York: McGraw-Hill.

9

The Montana Behavioral Initiative: A Statewide Response to Issues of School Violence

Mary Susan E. Fishbaugh
Montana State University–Billings

Joe Furshong
Helena Public Schools, Helena, MT

As the number of violent incidents involving school-age children increased in Montana and students with significant behavioral needs returned to their home schools from residential settings, Montana educators sought ways to ensure a safe school environment for all students. The result is the Montana Behavioral Initiative (MBI), a project that grew from five original sites in the 1995–1996 school year to more than 120 sites across the state during 1999–2000. The MBI is a comprehensive program involving staff development, schoolwide attitudinal changes toward student discipline, a commitment to problem solving, and ongoing technical assistance. Schools that adopt the MBI process improve their school environments through attention to the five key indicators of MBI and document continuing school improvement using the MBI Environmental Scan.

BACKGROUND: VIOLENCE IN MONTANA

Montana is a geographically vast state, ranking 4th in size but only 44th in population among the 50 United States. If superimposed on the eastern United States, Montana would stretch from Chicago in the west to Washington, DC, on the eastern seaboard, and from the southern Great Lakes to northern Tennessee. This vast expanse, however, is sparse in population, even with a recent influx of immigrants attracted by space, beautiful scenery, and lower land values. In fact, as a result of the 1990 census, Montana lost one of two congressional representatives. Even with an increase in population of over 100,000 as documented by the 2000 census, Montana has not grown enough to regain representation. Billings is the largest city in Montana with a population of approximately 100,000 inhabitants. Yellowstone County, of which Billings is the seat, has a total population of only 126,000. Billings is the largest city within a 500-mile radius. Salt Lake City and Denver to the south, Minneapolis to the east, and Spokane to the west are the nearest population centers.

Even with its Big Sky, vast prairies, and ample elbow room, Montana has its share of violence. Butte was one of the first communities to experience tragedy, when a young student opened fire on an elementary school playground, killing a classmate. The notorious Unabomber lived near Helena, the Montana capital. The freemen, an antigovernment right-wing group, were under siege by the FBI near Jordan. A man from Rimini opened fire in the U.S. Congress and killed two guards. Montana leads the nation in per-capita hunters and gun ownership.

Youth violence in Montana reflects a sort of Wild West mentality. A January 1998 United Way Community Indicators Report demonstrated that although juvenile nonviolent crime showed little change or decreased, assault by juveniles rose. The number of youth driving-under-the-influence (DUI) decreased, but youth drug charges increased. The number of youth arrested for carrying a concealed weapon rose. Similarly, a report from the Billings police department showed that whereas initial juvenile arrests decreased slightly from 1,341 in 1995 to 1,143 in 1997, total juvenile arrests rose sharply, from 1,160 to 2,104.

The Billings schools, similar to many schools throughout the country, experience increasing incidents of student misbehavior and more serious forms of inappropriate school behavior than in the past (United Way, 1998). Across the four high schools, truancy and unexcused absences are the most prevalent causes for student disciplinary referral. General noncompliance ranks third. The district reports significant numbers of incidents of defiance, disrespect, fighting, and harassment. Drug abuse/possession is more prevalent than is abuse or possession of alcohol. The district disciplined 11 students for carrying a weapon in school.

The four middle schools in the Billings district report similar types of unacceptable behavior. The fact that more middle school than high school students were disciplined for fighting, harassment, and weapons possession underscores the need for early and consistent behavioral intervention. The middle schools disciplined 25 students for drug possession, and 15 students for carrying a weapon.

School violence rates in Billings mirror national statistics. Results from a 1995 study conducted by the Centers for Disease Control indicated that 11.8% of the students surveyed had carried weapons in the previous month, 6.2% had been in a fight within the previous year, and 4.4% had skipped school at least 1 day in the previous month because they felt unsafe. The rate at which students drop out of high school has become a national concern.

Results of the Montana Youth Risk Behavior Survey (MBI Advisory Council, 1997; MBI Task Force, 1995, 1996; Office of Public Instruction, 1995) indicated even higher levels of the aforementioned incidents within the state of Montana. Twenty-three percent of Montana students surveyed had carried a weapon to school within the last 30 days, and 35% reported being in a fight within the last year. Montana's violent youth death rate ranks 11th highest in the nation; the rate for juveniles in custody is 14th in the country; and the state has the 5th highest teenage suicide rate. During the 1994–1995 school year, 19 students were expelled for bringing a firearm to school. Nearly 30% of the total reported arrests in the state are individuals under the age of 18.

Students with disabilities are not immune to violence. The literature is replete with studies concerning the social and behavioral skills of students with disabilities (Bender & J. K. Smith, 1990; Gresham, MacMillan, & Bocian, 1996; Larrivee & Horne, 1991; Sabornie, Marshall, & Ellis, 1990). These studies indicate that students with disabilities have lower self-concepts, are not accepted by their peers, and have behavioral problems in general-education classrooms. According to the U.S. Department of Education's *Sixteenth Annual Report to Congress* (1994), 50% of students identified as emotionally disturbed (ED), 32% of students with learning disabilities (LD), and 29% of students with mental retardation (MR) dropped out of school. This compares to 24% of the general school population who leave school before completion.

The number of students identified as having emotional disabilities in the state of Montana increased by 55.3% from 623 students during the 1988–1989 school year to 1,126 students in 1995–1996 (MBI Task Force, 1995). Children as young as 5 years ($N = 4$) were identified as having an emotional disorder in 1995, and the number of identified students increased with age. The greatest increase (72.7%) was between the ages of 11 ($N = 96$) and 12 ($N = 132$). By age 15 the number peaked at 174. As students reached the age when they could choose not to attend school, the number decreased with 137 students at age 16, 111 students at age 17, 43 students at age 18, and 10 students at age 19. Based on the statistics from the *Sixteenth Annual Report to Congress* (U.S. Department of Education, 1994) and other studies (Kortering & Blackorby, 1992), we might ask whether these students are exiting special-education programs or prematurely exiting school.

The MBI is a comprehensive staff development program created to improve the capacity of schools and communities to meet the diverse and increasingly complex social, emotional, and behavioral needs of students. The initiative assists educators to develop attitudes, skills, and systems necessary to help each student leave public education with the social competence for succeeding in society and the workplace. The MBI is consistent with the work of Kohn (1996), who suggested addressing student behavior from the perspective of building a community of respect, rather than from that of compliance to authority, and with the work of Johnson and Johnson (1995), who developed cooperative strategies for mediating student conflict. The MBI works to stem the violence continuum in schools (see Fig. 9.1 for an explanation of the violence continuum).

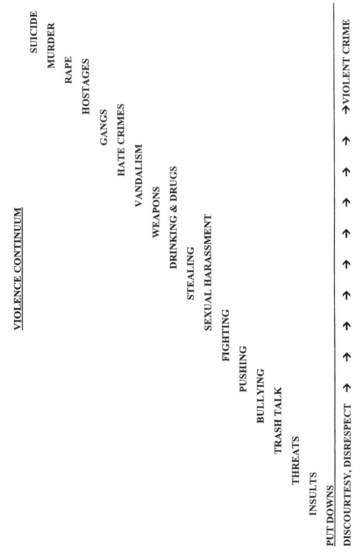

FIG. 9.1.   Violence continuum (Bryngelson & Cline, 1998).

THE MONTANA BEHAVIORAL INITIATIVE: A STATEWIDE RESPONSE

What the MBI Is

The MBI builds safe school environments through school–community collaboration and direct student instruction. Training in three areas—attitudes, skills, and systems—provides the context in which MBI works. MBI expands on current programs at the elementary, middle, and high schools by using an organized team effort and by focusing on development of a respectful school environment.

Five schools became model MBI sites in the spring of 1995. Each site selected a team of educators, parents, and community people who participated in a week long MBI summer institute. The institute focused on a variety of behavioral interventions and approaches to promoting positive school culture. Each team assessed the needs in their school and community, proposed goals to address those needs, developed strategies designed to meet the goals, and planned for evaluation. Since 1995, MBI has spread across Montana and interest in the process continues to grow (see Fig. 9.2 for a map of MBI sites.)

Theoretical Basis

Previous Theory and Research. The Iowa Behavioral Initiative and effective schools research form the basis of MBI. Two simultaneously oc-

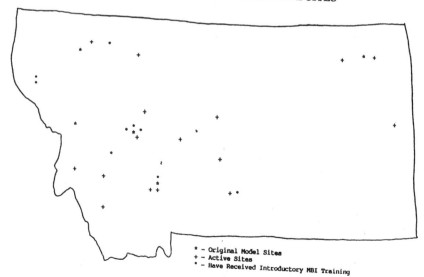

FIG. 9.2. Map of Montana Behavioral Initiative sites.

curring phenomena—increasing violence in Montana schools and lack of residential placements for students with behavioral disorders—precipitated the Office of Public Instruction to search for possible solutions. Impressed with efforts made by the state of Iowa to address similar concerns, Montana modeled its behavioral initiative on a successful Iowa program. Iowa's initiative built school cultures to foster social, emotional, and behavioral success for all students, but in particular for students at risk of school failure, dropping out, and escalating unacceptable behavior. Montana adopted Iowa project strategies—organizing a school MBI team, establishing a school safety baseline, and determining site-specific goals (MBI Task Force, 1995). Montana enhanced the behavioral initiative through use of trained regional consultants available to offer technical assistance or professional coaching to site teams.

Philosophically, MBI is compatible with effective schools research (Owens, 1995; Purkey & M. C. Smith, 1985). Each of the following components is common to both:

- Effective programs and schools have unconditional positive regard for students, maintain a positive/proactive focus, assert beliefs of responsibility and self-efficacy, and affirm high, success-oriented student expectations.
- Effective programs and schools match instruction/services to individual student needs, employ direct-instruction social-skills curricula, use validated instructional strategies, and provide systematic, data-based interventions.
- Effective systems are supported by strong leaders, provide an array of services, engage parents, collaborate with a variety of caregivers, employ schoolwide approaches involving both general and special educators, engage in thoughtfully planned staff development for school improvement, and conduct ongoing program evaluation.

MBI incorporates the *positive behavior support* process (Weigle, 1997). Positive behavior support includes basic tenets such as broad emphasis, long-term goals, individual effectiveness, direct teaching of skills, and multi-component intervention.

The MBI adopted *Foundations: Establishing Positive Discipline Policies* (Sprick, 1995) and *School-Wide Discipline: Developing a Curriculum of Responsibility* (Garrison, 1996) as the bases for site discipline policy and strategies. Initially, results of three surveys determine perceptions of school safety, faculty-to-student interactions, and student-to-student interactions. One survey seeks this information from staff, another from students, and the third from parents. Site-specific goals to address school safety issues and strategies for goal achievement are based on survey results.

MBI Goals and Process

MBI Goals.   Montana Behavioral Initiative goals include the following:

- Recognize and create community/school programs that effectively meet the needs of students and develop safe, orderly environments.
- Improve the willingness of school and community personnel to respond proactively to the individual student needs.
- Extend the range and quality of services available to students ensuring they have social competence.
- Provide school and community personnel with validated strategies for responding proactively to challenging behavior and teaching social competence.
- Strengthen the ability of schools and community agencies to network and coordinate community resources.
- Modify school and community agency policies and procedures to facilitate more effective and efficient services for youth.

MBI Process.   In order to achieve these goals, MBI employs a process with the following components:

- Develop a school team including but not limited to a general educator, a special educator, an administrator, a parent, and a community agency representative.
- Implement a structured team process by meeting regularly as documented through agendas and minutes.
- Develop school vision and mission statements and post throughout the school building.
- Develop a school responsibility plan and post throughout the building.

Each MBI team develops vision and mission statements for their site and facilitates adoption of the statements as policy by the school faculty and staff as a whole. Based on the site vision and mission, the team develops guidelines for success that serve as general school rules for promoting responsible student behavior. The team facilitates faculty/staff determination of roles and responsibilities for school implementation. The team then facilitates site development of techniques for acknowledging responsible choices, and for correcting irresponsible behavior. Usually, teams begin implementing the curriculum and site-specific strategies in common areas such as the lunchroom, halls, playground/parking lot, and bus areas. These are the least structured/supervised areas, thus recognized as being least safe. Current MBI sites in Montana have documented significant growth toward their site goals using positive discipline policies and a curriculum of responsibility.

A site facilitator monitors MBI progress at each school. One person is trained as the MBI team leader. After attending the annual MBI summer institute, the lead team member participates in two additional days of facilitator training and attends follow-up training scheduled during the school year. Facilitator responsibilities include:

- Convening team meetings and maintaining meeting agendas and minutes.
- Overseeing the survey process including distribution, data analysis, and dissemination of results
- Publishing the school vision and mission statements.
- Providing school responsibility plans for each classroom teacher at the site.
- Guiding the team in maintaining the MBI Environment Scan.

Components

Components of MBI include an annual summer institute, site teams, ongoing technical assistance, program evaluation, information dissemination, and governance by the MBI Advisory Council.

State MBI Summer Institute. Each summer since 1995, MBI offers a 5-day institute for site team development and training. National leaders in the areas of teaming, proactive discipline, safe schools, and community building/outreach (e.g., Howard Adelman & Linda Taylor, Geoffrey Colvin, Scott Poland, Randall Sprick, George Sugai, and Jesus Villahermosa) present information to prepare site personnel for MBI implementation. Teams learn the importance of the school–community partnership in meeting student behavioral needs. Team members extend their knowledge with regard to best practices and share strategies for working with challenging students. Teams adopt a problem-solving approach for building a safe school environment. The institute provides a structure for continual exchange of information and sharing of successful practice. Summer training allows team members to lead their school in implementing effective practice.

Technical Assistance. Recognizing the importance of continuing support following initial training, MBI provides technical assistance to school teams in two ways. The first, described earlier, is the individual site facilitator who receives preparation beyond the MBI Summer institute and leads the site team as they implement the MBI process at their school.

The second form of technical assistance is provided by five MBI consultants, a small, highly trained cadre. Roughly organized by regions of the state, MBI consultants provide regional, community, or building-specific technical assistance as needed.

Interagency Cooperation. An essential component of the MBI process is interagency cooperation. Site teams work with other community agencies and service providers to provide a comprehensive community service continuum. Persons from community agencies, invited to be members of site teams, attend the summer institute, and share MBI information with their professional constituencies. Head Start staff, mental health providers, private counselors, social workers, probation officers, and school resource officers are examples of community representatives on school MBI teams.

Program Evaluation. Since the inception of MBI, program evaluation has been a priority. Each year, a comprehensive evaluation of the Summer Institute is conducted. During the first year of program implementation, site teams maintained logs, kept record of meeting dates with agendas and minutes, reported data resulting from site surveys, and followed one at-risk student who might benefit from the MBI. During the second year, sites maintained data with regard to site-specified goals. Six project evaluation reports—four reports reviewing the first four Summer Institutes, and two annual reports documenting model-site activity and progress—are available for review. Beginning with the 1997–1998 school year, any school attempting to implement MBI has maintained the Environmental Scan (see Appendix).

Gathering evaluation information that is consistent is challenging. Because the various MBI components are not mandated, but tailored to meet individual school needs, site evaluation reports vary. Some schools begin with a determined effort to produce initial data. Other schools decide against initial evaluation due to a variety of factors. Several years into MBI implementation, follow-up evaluation without initial baseline data proves to be difficult. The result has been accumulation of a massive body of anecdotal information describing MBI's positive impact, but fragmented and inconsistent hard data. The Environmental Scan, revised several times, now serves as both implementation guide and assessment device.

Information Dissemination. Information about MBI is disseminated throughout the year in a variety of ways. The project has an informational brochure that is distributed at state and regional professional meetings and conferences. Site personnel are invited to make presentations at non-MBI schools. Personnel from other schools are welcome to visit current MBI sites. Networking among professionals within the state is an informal means of "getting the word out." Attendance at the MBI summer institute has increased from five teams in 1995 to 750 participants in 2000. Three hundred individuals new to MBI attended the MBI Institute in June 2000 along with 450 returning MBI team members. Although "the word is out," the ultimate goal of MBI is to move beyond information dissemination to diffusion and adoption of the MBI philosophy and process throughout Montana.

Governance.   Since December of 1997, the MBI has been governed by an interagency MBI Advisory Council. Initially the Council included four subcommittees—Budget/Finance Committee, Program Development/Dissemination Committee, Community Involvement Committee, and Public Relations Committee. Ad hoc, issue-based committees have replaced the initial standing committees. The regionally based MBI consultants, available for technical assistance to school sites, serve as a work group to carry out ongoing planning tasks.

Funding.   MBI began in 1995 with a 2-year grant from the Montana State School Boards Association in conjunction with the Board of Crime Control. Funding was continued for an additional 2 years. However, the Budget/Finance Committee was unsuccessful in securing further funding from the Montana State Legislature. Currently, the Montana Office of Public Instruction, Special Education Division supports MBI through discretionary funds.

RESULTS

Each MBI site exemplifies five MBI Key Indicators as detailed on the Environmental Scan:
- Continuing Education and Training.
- Structured Team Process.
- Best Practices Curricular Approach to Behavioral Support.
- Ongoing Evaluation Efforts.
- Community Involvement.

MBI sites are instructed in use of the Environmental Scan as an implementation guide and as a program assessment device during the Summer Institute. MBI Consultants offer ongoing assistance, as needed, as teams attempt to use the Scan.

The second annual project report (Fishbaugh, 1997) documented accomplishments by the original five MBI school sites. The Executive Summary of the report demonstrated wide variety in individual team goals and strategies, as well as accomplishments:

- Bozeman—Teachers reported spending less time on student discipline as a result of MBI. The overwhelming majority of teachers (97%) and students (88%) understood and accepted their school rules. Discipline became consistent throughout individual schools.
- Helena—One Helena middle school targeted two common areas for reducing misbehavior referrals. Referrals from the lunchroom dropped 63%; hallway referrals dropped 86%; referrals for physical confrontations dropped 56%; and verbal confrontations dropped 100%.

- Missoula—As a result of the MBI survey on school safety, a Missoula middle school drafted a policy supporting school staff in coming to consensus with regard to student expected behavior, and encouraging all school staff to feel responsible for all students. Responsible behavior was no longer left to individual definitions or to not-so-common "common sense."
- Whitefish—Focus at this site was on three goals: playground incidents, rough play, and hallway infractions. Students performed skits describing inappropriate and appropriate behavior. As a result, both students and staff became sensitive to behavioral expectations.
- Wolf Point—One elementary school maintained detailed records on three at-risk students. From the first 6-week period to the third, negative incidents involving a fourth grader dropped from 19 to 3. During the same period, negative incidents involving a fifth grader dropped from 39 to 13. Negative incidents involving a sixth grader decreased from 39 to 26. An increase in referrals to the school principal for positive behavior reflected system change in overall discipline philosophy.

THE FUTURE OF MBI

The MBI grew from an initial five model sites to over 120 during the 1999–2000 school year. The phenomenal growth of this project has made both project coordination and evaluation efforts challenging. With numerous anecdotal reports of success, however, interest in MBI as a means for preventing and addressing difficult behavior in schools continues to grow. The sixth annual MBI Summer Institute was held in June 2000 with seven strands to meet information and training needs of both new and returning participants.

The MBI Consultants have become the backbone of the project. These five individuals assist with the summer institute, train site facilitators, make MBI informational presentations for interested schools, offer ongoing technical assistance on an as-needed basis, and lead evaluation efforts. Through their dedication and insight, the Environmental Scan has been revised and incorporated as an essential component for any school claiming MBI status. Employed by urban school districts or rural special-education cooperatives, the consultants' MBI work is in addition to their usual professional responsibilities.

MBI is a multistep process that incorporates a structured team approach to schoolwide discipline changes. MBI involves multiple levels—local, regional, and state constituencies—in order to be effective. It is this comprehensive, systemic approach coupled with the vision, spirit, and hard work of MBI leaders that have led to the MBI being Montana's statewide response to school safety issues.

CHAPTER ACTIVITIES

For Discussion

1.   Although Montana is a rural state, Bozeman is growing, as is the capital, Helena. Both Bozeman and Helena adopted MBI for all schools throughout their districts.

- List the components of MBI and discuss the applicability of each to rural and to urban schools.

2.   Describe student behavioral problems that your school faces.

- What strategies are you using to address the problems?
- What are your results?

3.   Have you encountered, through your reading or professional conference attendance, programs similar to MBI.

- Describe the program(s).
- Compare and contrast with MBI.

Case Study

For this case, describe your school. Is it elementary, secondary or perhaps postsecondary? How many students, faculty, staff? What are the general demographics of the school—location, socioeconomic status, age of facility? What about student behavioral issues? What is the philosophy of student discipline? How is discipline handled and by whom? How do the students feel about the process?

1. Refer to the Appendix. Complete the MBI Environmental Scan with reference to your school.
2. What first steps might you take to strengthen your school's current practice or to begin changing your school from an adversarial environment to an environment of respect?

REFERENCES

Bender, W. N., & Smith, J. K. (1990). Classroom behavior of children and adolescents with learning disabilities: A meta-analysis. *Journal of Learning Disabilities, 23,* 298–305.

Bryngelson, J., & Cline, S. (1998). *A Violence Continuum.* Billings, MT: CARE.

Fishbaugh, M. S. E. (1997). *MBI 1996/97 evaluation report.* Billings: Montana State University.

Garrison, M. (Presenter). (1996). *School-wide discipline: Developing a curriculum of responsibility.* Roseburg, OR: Educational Support Services.

Gresham, F. M., MacMillan, D. L., & Bocian, K. (1997). "Behavioral earthquakes": Low frequency, salient behavioral events that differentiate students at-risk for behavioral disorders. *Behavioral Disorders, 21*(4), 277–292.

Johnson, D. W., & Johnson, R. T. (1995). *Reducing school violence through conflict resolution.* Alexandria, VA: Association for Supervision and Curriculum Development.

Kohn, A. (1996). *Beyond discipline: From compliance to community.* Alexandria, VA: Association for Supervision and Curriculum Development.

Kortering, L. J., & Blackorby, J. (1992). High school dropout and students identified with behavioral disorders. *Behavioral Disorders, 18*, 24–32.

Larrivee, B., & Horne, M. (1991). Social status: A comparison of mainstreamed students with peers of different ability levels. *The Journal of Special Education, 25*(1), 90–101.

MBI Advisory Council. (1997). *Montana Behavioral Initiative community model site project.* Unpublished grant proposal.

MBI Task Force. (1995). *Montana Behavioral Initiative community model site project.* Unpublished grant proposal.

MBI Task Force. (1996). *Montana Behavior Initiative.* [Presentation overheads]. Helena, MT: Author.

Office of Public Instructions. (1995). *Montana youth risk behavior survey summary report.* Helena, MT: Author.

Owens, R. G. (1995). *Organizational behavior in education.* Boston: Allyn & Bacon.

Purkey, S. C., & Smith, M. S. (1985). School reform: The district policy implications of the effective schools literature. *The Elementary School Journal, 85*, 353–89.

Sabornie, E., Marshall, J., & Ellis, E. (1990). Restructuring of mainstream sociometry with learning disabled and nonhandicapped students. *Exceptional Children, 56*(4), 314,323.

Sprick, R. (Presenter). (1995). *Foundations: Establishing positive discipline policies.* Eugene, OR: Teaching Strategies, Inc.

United Way of Yellowstone County. (1998). *Community indicator's report.* Billings, MT: Author.

U.S. Department of Education. (1994). *To assure the free appropriate public education of all children with disabilities: Sixteenth annual report to Congress on the implementation of The Individuals With Disabilities Education Act.* Washington, DC: Author.

Weigle, K. L. (1997). Positive behavior support as a model for promoting educational inclusion. *The Journal of the Association for Persons With Severe Handicaps, 22*(1), 36–48.

Appendix

MBI

MONTANA BEHAVIORAL INITIATIVE

Document of Participation

We, the MBI Team for _____ School do make a commitment to incorporate the following essential components to the Montana Behavioral Initiative at our school. In so doing, we are making a good faith effort to exemplify the mission, principles, and goals of the Montana Behavioral Initiative, ensuring a positive school environment in which the students of our community can grow and learn.

MBI KEY INDICATORS

1. MBI Training
2. MBI Team Process
3. Proactive Support Systems Approach Using Best Practices
4. Evaluation Process
5. Community Process

MBI Environmental Scan — To be completed, monitored, and maintained by the site team.

MBI Annual Initiative Participation — A team representing the school will attend each summer institute. The members may vary.

MBI Facilitator Training — Each school will designate one team member as facilitator. The facilitator will attend annual training for 1 year.

Site Administrator/Principle	Date	MBI Team Member	Date
MBI Team Member	Date	MBI Team Facilitator	Date
MBI Team Member	Date	MBI Team Member	Date

MONTANA BEHAVIORAL INITIATIVE
ENVIRONMENTAL SCAN

MBI SITE _____   DATE _____

The Montana Behavioral Initiative (MBI) is a comprehensive staff development process designed to facilitate school system and attitudinal changes for addressing increasingly complex needs of today's students. Through the MBI, Montana hopes to provide the structure and knowledge necessary for assisting schools with improving school climate and classroom environments in order to meet the needs of children with behavioral challenges. The term "initiative" refers to proactive efforts by schools to identify priority concerns involving school safety and to teach alternative acceptable behaviors. Community involvement and statewide networking are essential to the MBI. Beginning with five model sites in 1995, MBI has grown to include schools and communities throughout Montana.

Five key indicators characterize MBI Programs: **1. MBI Training 2. MBI Team Process 3. Proactive Support Systems Approach Using Best Practices 4. Evaluation Process and 5. Community Process.** School sites document their progress in the MBI Process by maintaining the Environmental Scan. Each MBI site should view the scan in light of the following two considerations: 1. Individual MBI teams determine site needs, make program decisions, and document success based on systematically collected data. 2. Individual MBI teams develop strategies and select procedures appropriate for their school.

INSTRUCTIONS: Select the numerical rating that best represents your school's implementation of each MBI Key Indicator.
(Unless stated, MBI does **not require all** components for each indicator.) Indicate on the form what data have been collected and attach data summaries and samples.

- **0**   Not selected for implementation
- **1**   Started but abandoned
- **2**   Planned for implementation (to begin int he future)
- **3**   Emergent implementation (started)
- **4**   Implementation being refined/revised (reviewing what is happening)
- **5**   Implementation completed
- •   Implementation data collected

MBI Training

Goal: To increase the awareness and understanding of effective schools practices

	PROCESS CONTINUUM						DOCUMENTATION	
	Not Selected	Abandoned	Planned	Emergent	Revised	Implemented	Date	Attach Copies
1. MBI Team Training								
Site facilitator selected and trained			2	3	4	5		
Team members attend summer institute (# attend)			2	3	4	5		
Team members understand the key indicators and philosophy of MBI			2	3	4	5		
2. MBI Building- and/or District-Level Staff Training								
Staff development activities to address MBI philosophy/ background			2	3	4	5		
MBI facilitator/team provides ongoing information on MBI to school staff			2	3	4	5		
MBI facilitator/team provides overview of MBI to school board	0	1	2	3	4	5		
MBI facilitator/team provides orientation of MBI to school district	0	1	2	3	4	5		
MBI facilitator/team provides orientation of MBI to community/ parent group(s)	0	1	2	3	4	5		

MBI Team Process

Goal: To increase and improve the use of team processes in educational decision-making and in addressing issues concerning our youth

	PROCESS CONTINUUM						DOCUMENTATION	
1. Administrative Commitment to MBI Process	Not Selected	Abandoned	Planned	Emergent	Revised	Implemented	Date	Attach Copies
Administrative support via commitment letter and behavior (e.g., release time, in-service training to staff, respect for team decisions)			2	3	4	5		
MBI team established			2	3	4	5		
2. Site-Specific Goals and Implementation Strategies Developed								
Mission statement developed and publicized	0	1	2	3	4	5		
Vision statement developed and publicized	0	1	2	3	4	5		
Guidelines for success/code of conducts/behavior expectations developed, taught, and publicized	0	1	2	3	4	5		
Evaluation information used to develop goals and strategies	0	1	2	3	4	5		

continued on next page

167

MBI Team Process (*continued*)

	PROCESS CONTINUUM						DOCUMENTATION	
	Not Selected	Abandoned	Planned	Emergent	Revised	Implemented	Date	Attach Copies
Site-based goal developed	0	1	2	3	4	5		
Research-based interventions strategies selected to accomplish goals	0	1	2	3	4	5		
Implementation and evaluation timeline established	0	1	2	3	4	5		
3. Team-Building Activities								
Team receives in-service on the team process, modification, and evaluation activities	0	1	2	3	4	5		
Team meeting occur on a regular basis with consistent attendance			2	3	4	5		
Implementation and evaluation timeline established	0	1	2	3	4	5		

Proactive Support Systems Approach Using Best Practices

Goal: To support the implementation of best practices procedures in Montana's schools, foster beliefs that hold that all children are valued, and that positive and proactive approaches to problems produce the most satisfying results

1. School-Wide	PROCESS CONTINUUM						DOCUMENTATION	
	Not Selected	Abandoned	Planned	Emergent	Revised	Implemented	Date	Attach Copies
Physical plant has been considered in terms of safety and climate, to minimize problems	0	1	2	3	4	5		
Climate-building activities identified and implemented	0	1	2	3	4	5		
Increase in positive interactions between staff and students	0	1	2	3	4	5		
All students and staff familiar with expectations for behavior	0	1	2	3	4	5		
Staff demonstrates knowledge of a variety of proactive intervention strategies and intervene early	0	1	2	3	4	5		
Staff implements procedures to teach expected behaviors to students	0	1	2	3	4	5		
Ongoing in-service training available to staff	0	1	2	3	4	5		
Other	0	1	2	3	4	5		

continued on next page

Proactive Support Systems Approach Using Best Practices   (continued)

	PROCESS CONTINUUM						DOCUMENTATION	
	Not Selected	Abandoned	Planned	Emergent	Revised	Implemented	Date	Attach Copies
2. Nonclassroom								
Evaluation data have been reviewed to determine what support system needs to be in place in noninstructional settings	0	1	2	3	4	5		
"Responsibility Plans" have been developed for one or more noninstructional settings	0	1	2	3	4	5		
Plans taught and reviewed on a regular basis	0	1	2	3	4	5		
Staff supervision has increased in common areas	0	1	2	3	4	5		
Staff has knowledge of key staff behaviors that affect student management	0	1	2	3	4	5		
Other	0	1	2	3	4	5		
3. Social-skills instruction taking place								
Teacher support teams utilized (e.g., Intervention Assistance Team)	0	1	2	3	4	5		
Classroom expectations are taught	0	1	2	3	4	5		

Proactive Support Systems Approach Using Best Practices *(continued)*

	PROCESS CONTINUUM						DOCUMENTATION	
	Not Selected	Abandoned	Planned	Emergent	Revised	Implemented	Date	Attach Copies
Classroom climate—building activities developed and implemented	0	1	2	3	4	5		
Instructional strategies adjusted to individual student needs	0	1	2	3	4	5		
Other	0	1	2	3	4	5		
4. Individual Student								
Effective support system in place to meet needs of teachers/students concerning challenging behaviors (e.g., counseling, consultation, alternative ed. sites, interagency)	0	1	2	3	4	5		
Crisis plans developed	0	1	2	3	4	5		
Functional assessments and positive behavior strategies utilized to meet individual student needs	0	1	2	3	4	5		
Individualized intervention plans employed to meet individual student needs	0	1	2	3	4	5		

(continued on next page)

Proactive Support Systems Approach Using Best Practices *(continued)*

	PROCESS CONTINUUM						DOCUMENTATION	
	Not Selected	Abandoned	Planned	Emergent	Revised	Implemented	Date	Attach Copies
Other	0	1	2	3	4	5		
5. Family								
School team has conducted MBI awareness activities with families/parents	0	1	2	3	4	5		
School team has included parents in aspects of MBI training, planning, or implementation	0	1	2	3	4	5		
Other	0	1	2	3	4	5		

Evaluation Process

Goal: To increase the awareness of the value and use of data-based decision making in education

1. Mandatory	PROCESS CONTINUUM						DOCUMENTATION	
	Not Selected	Abandoned	Planned	Emergent	Revised	Implemented	Date	Attach Copies
Environmental scan completed/submitted which documents forward progress toward MBI goals and objectives			2	3	4	5		
Surveys conducted with all school staff (e.g., teachers, janitors, paraeducators, students, office, lunchroom personnel, etc.)			2	3	4	5		
Observations completed: • Faculty behavior • Student behavior			2	3	4	5		
Incident records, suspension/expulsion data collected			2	3	4	5		
Systematic review of existing policies conducted			2	3	4	5		
Objectives and intervention plans developed from data			2	3	4	5		
Effectiveness of proactive strategies/interventions determined			2	3	4	5		
Mission, vision, and guidelines for success reviewed and revised as needed	0	1	2	3	4	5		
Site log maintained (i.e., record of agendas and minutes)			2	3	4	5		

Evaluation Process

Goal: To increase the awareness of the value and use of data-based decision making in education

1. Optional	PROCESS CONTINUUM						DOCUMENTATION	
	Not Selected	Abandoned	Planned	Emergent	Revised	Implemented	Date	Attach Copies
Other observations and/or functional assessments	0	1	2	3	4	5		
Other records (truancy, tardies, drop-out rates, Title IX, referrals, mobility rates, etc.)	0	1	2	3	4	5		
Utilize Phase 1, 2, or 3 checklists	0	1	2	3	4	5		

Community Process
(Not a Required Element at this time)

Goal: To foster the belief that the education of today's youth is a community responsibility

1. Training	PROCESS CONTINUUM						DOCUMENTATION	
	Not Selected	Abandoned	Planned	Emergent	Revised	Implemented	Date	Attach Copies
MBI facilitators trained in steps to achieve community involvement	0	1	2	3	4	5		
School-based MBI Team constructs "Community Assets Map"	0	1	2	3	4	5		
Community needs identified	0	1	2	3	4	5		
MBI awareness activities held / surveys conducted	0	1	2	3	4	5		
Intervention planning follow-up meetings held	0	1	2	3	4	5		
Implement plan	0	1	2	3	4	5		
Measure outcomes	0	1	2	3	4	5		

Author Index

Subject Index

M